STARTING FROM THE CHILD

SECOND EDITION

STARTING FROM THE CHILD

Teaching and learning from 3 to 8

SECOND EDITION

JULIE FISHER

Open University Press
Buckingham · Philadelphia

Open University Press
Celtic Court
22 Ballmoor
Buckingham
MK18 1XW

email: enquiries@openup.co.uk
world wide web: www.openup.co.uk

and
325 Chestnut Street
Philadelphia, PA 19106, USA

First edition published 1996
Reprinted 1998 (twice), 1999, 2000
First published in this second edition 2002

A catalogue record of this book is available from the British Library

ISBN   0 335 20918 1 (pb)

Library of Congress Cataloging-in-Publication Data
Fisher, Julie, 1950-
    Starting from the child? : teaching and learning from 3 to 8 /
Julie Fisher. – 2nd ed.
        p.   cm.
    Includes bibliographical references and index.
    ISBN 0-335-20918-1 (pbk.)
        1. Early childhood education.   2. Learning, Psychology of.   I. Title.

LB1139.23 F57 2001
372.21–dc21   2001021069

Typeset by Graphicraft Limited, Hong Kong
Printed in Great Britain by Crommell Press Limited, Trowbridge

to Paula,
whose classroom practice inspired this book

CONTENTS

LIST OF BOXES AND FIGURES

PREFACE TO THE SECOND EDITION

I wrote the first edition of *Starting from the Child?* in 1996. It was a time of great uncertainty for many practitioners in early childhood education and I was feeling this uncertainty as much as others. I had recently left headship and had seen, in my last few months in that job, the introduction of the National Curriculum and national testing. There was an instant and obvious pressure on the learning entitlement and experience of the young children in my school and it seemed that early childhood educators faced increasing pressure from above as the full weight of attainment targets, levels and national testing bore down on the youngest children. I moved on to a role in initial teacher education at the University of Reading and these downward pressures continued to be apparent. Opportunities for students training to be teachers in nursery and infant schools to study how children develop and how they learn were squeezed in favour of more subject and curriculum knowledge, which was deemed to be a more desirable pedagogy.

Then external agendas focused specifically on early childhood. The government introduced vouchers to fund universal preschool provision (erroneously called 'nursery' provision) for 4-year-olds, and established goals (Desirable Learning Outcomes) for children to work towards by the time they entered school. Demonstrating value-added performance became increasingly important and it was not long before baseline assessment on entry to primary schooling was introduced as a benchmark against which children's early progress could be judged.

In a few short years, early childhood educators have seen play vilified and then promoted as 'a key way in which young children learn with enjoyment and challenge' (QCA/DfEE 2000); fought to keep personal and social education as a core element of the early years curriculum and then found four aims of the Foundation Stage dedicated to it; campaigned for early years to be recognized as a specialism and then found the government crying out for specialist teachers, not only for nursery and reception classes, but to work alongside and improve the quality of the curriculum in the non-maintained sector.

Holding resolutely to the principles of early childhood education has borne fruit. For all of us it has been essential that practitioners have managed to demonstrate the power of those principles in practice. Those early childhood educators who have continued to put observation of children's learning at the heart of their practice, to document children's learning meticulously and to plan a curriculum that is flexible and responsive, have provided the evidence that this remains the best way to deliver appropriately differentiated, challenging and effective education in the early years. Such an educational experience does not exclude adult-initiated activities, it does not reject whole class teaching or ignore the importance of skills in literacy and numeracy. It does, however, set these in a proper context – the context of each child's uniqueness as a learner. The national thrust towards setting targets for individual children is no more and no less than child-centred education. It is knowing the child well through observation, assessing their current skills and understandings, making a judgement about their potential learning within their zone of proximal development and setting a challenge for them to learn through carefully planned learning experiences. This is what good nursery teachers have always done and no strategy, no format, no one-size-fits-all curriculum can adequately replace this process.

Young children are active, interactive, dynamic and ravenous learners. If they are presented with learning environments and situations that do not satisfy their hunger then their learning becomes less enthusiastic and – worst of all – they may lose the appetite and desire to learn. In my current job I am privileged to watch children and young people of all ages engaged with their teachers in the process of learning. Nothing I have witnessed in classes for children from age 3 to 18 has challenged my conviction that effective education is one that starts from the child.

Consequently the time has come in this second edition to remove the question mark from the title of my book. I am no longer questioning whether one should, or can, begin an education starting from the child. It is an imperative.

ACKNOWLEDGEMENTS

So much of this book has been influenced by the principles and practice of colleagues with whom I have had the privilege to work. My sincere thanks go to Janet Moyles, who encouraged me to write and opened the doors for me to do so. I am grateful to Keith Postlethwaite, at the University of Reading, who read my early work, took it seriously and gave me the confidence to continue. I am particularly indebted to both Angela Redfern and Carol Boulter who accepted the time-consuming role of 'critical friend' and helped so much to challenge and refine my thinking and writing. My thanks go to my colleagues in the Early Years Curriculum Group have read and commented on chapters of this book and have been a constant source of inspiration. My thanks also to Tina Bruce for her thought-provoking and supportive comments. I am privileged to be part of the Oxfordshire Early Years Team, and I am grateful to all my colleagues for the generous way in which they share their experiences, their ideas, their enthusiasm and their friendship. Finally, my loving thanks to David, who listens endlessly while I rehearse my ideas and gives me the time and space to put them into practice.

1

COMPETENT YOUNG LEARNERS

What children know and can do

Introduction

Before children come to school at the age of 5 they have developed a range of skills, knowledge and understanding at a speed that will never again be repeated in their lives. The years from 0 to 7 are a period in human development when the capacity to learn is, in John Brierley's words (1994) 'at flood-readiness'. All the evidence shows that, in their early years, young children demonstrate a variety of characteristics which make them natural and successful learners. However, when those same children arrive at school it can be a different story. Children who have been motivated and determined become disillusioned and disaffected (Barrett 1989; Smith 1995); children who made sense of things and had begun to form their own personal construct of the world become confused and disorientated (Donaldson 1978; 1992); children who posed a thousand and one questions become quiet and uncommunicative (Tizard and Hughes 1984; Cousins 1999). It seems that schooling can inhibit some of the most prominent characteristics of competent young learners.

Yet quite clearly it is the desire of all teachers to bring about learning, and their efforts to do so and the personal time and commitment they give to their task is not in question (Campbell *et al.* 1993). Despite changes in education policy which, in terms of speed and influence, are unparalleled in the history of the UK state education system (Pollard *et al.* 1994), most teachers have sustained their commitment to children and to their best interests (Woods 1990).

So how can there be such a gap between some children's learning before they begin at school and the learning that follows? Is it simply a question of ratios – too many children and not enough teachers – or is the reason more complex? It would seem that at the root of the dichotomy between learning and schooling lies a failure on the part of educationalists in general to learn from those who have been most successful in the teaching and learning process in the child's preschool years. If more time were spent observing the strategies of children as learners, prior to the constraints of schooling, and more notice taken of the strategies of the significant adults with whom children learn, then there might be more chance of schools mirroring the successes of children's earliest learning environments.

The influence of experience on heredity

If schools are to look more to the learning of children before they reach statutory school age, then it is necessary to understand children's development in those early years. The development of every child is the result of a unique interaction of experience with heredity. While genetic programming determines many of the characteristics displayed by any human being, a variety of environmental influences combine to affect the development of the brain and consequently the individual (Shaffer 1993). The balance between these two key factors varies within each child, but the impact of 'nurture' on 'nature' will determine the characteristics which differentiate one child from another and make his or her development unique. Hereditary influence means that given the same set of experiences, one child's abilities will differ from another's, irrespective of the experiences they have. Equally, a child raised in a particular set of environmental circumstances can have their genetic programming nullified and their hereditary advantages erased (Meadows 1993).

Until fairly recently, the emphasis in education has been to make up for the deficits of a poor set of hereditary circumstances (Anning 1991). In the 1960s and 1970s there was 'a naive belief that compensatory education would serve to combat the known effects of social disadvantage on children's educational achievements' (Anning 1991: 5). While many research studies have now discredited such assumptions, there is other evidence that highlights the negative effects on development of a poor set of environmental factors (e.g. Smith 1995). Mia Kellmer Pringle, the first director of the National Children's Bureau, identified four human basic needs which have to be met from 'the very beginning of life and continue to require fulfilment – to a greater or lesser extent – throughout adulthood' (1992: 34). In Chapter 2 she identifies:

- the need for love and security;
- the need for new experiences;
- the need for praise and recognition;
- the need for responsibility.

Jennie Lindon in her book on child development (1993: 11–12) also identifies some basic needs of young children:

- the need to be cared for physically;
- the need to be kept safe;
- the need for emotional well-being.

All of these needs have to be met by the caring adult if children are to thrive and make the most of their developmental opportunities. Research cited by the Carnegie Corporation of New York (1994) provides substantial evidence that *lack* of certain experiences, and inappropriate or impoverished environments in the early stages of learning, may have long lasting detrimental effects on the development of children. The report, drawing on research that illuminates the workings of the nervous system, highlights the critical importance of the first three years of life. The results of the research lead to five key findings which are of profound significance to all those who are concerned with the development and education of young children:

- brain development that takes place before age 1 is more rapid and extensive than previously realized;
- brain development is much more vulnerable to environmental influence than was ever suspected;
- the influence of early environment on brain development is long lasting;
- the environment affects not only the number of brain cells and number of connections among them, but also the way these connections are 'wired';
- there is new scientific evidence for the negative impact of early stress on brain function.

(Carnegie Corporation 1994: 7–9)

These findings give a clear rationale for creating environments that offer experiences sensitive to the needs of young children and appropriate to their development, because the results of these experiences – good or bad – stay with children forever. The fact that the effects of early experiences appear to be cumulative only adds to the need to safeguard the environmental influences determining the development of all young children:

> an adverse environment can compromise a young child's brain function and overall development, placing him or her at greater risk of developing a variety of cognitive, behavioral, and physical difficulties. In some cases these effects may be irreversible.
>
> (Carnegie Corporation 1994: xiii)

New understandings about brain development

Any perusal of literature and conference themes over the past five years will reveal a proliferation of interest in groundbreaking knowledge about the brain and its functioning. The implications of such research for educators and their understanding of the processes of learning are immense. There is consensus that more has been learnt about the brain during the 1990s than in all previous scientific history (Greenfield 1997; Pinker 1997; Rose and Nicholl 1997; Jenson 1998; Wolfe and Brandt 1998). By nine months gestation, human beings have most of the neurons (nerve endings) in their brains that they are ever likely to have (Greenfield 1997). At birth, a child's brain contains around 100 billion neurons, each with the capacity to contribute to that individual's knowledge and understanding of skills and concepts that will determine their unique growth and development (Pinker 1977; Bruer 1999). Of particular importance to those in early education is the evidence that it is not the *number* of brain cells that is important, but how they become connected to each other that makes them effective (Greenfield 1997; Diamond and Hopson 1998). It is the use to which the neurons are put that determines the growth of a brain's functions (Calvin 1996). Growing neurons can adapt sensitively to changing circumstances in order to make the best of a situation (Greenfield 1997) but the key to growth is whether the neurons are sufficiently stimulated to make contact with other neurons and make a firm connection (Cohen 1997; Diamond and Hopson 1998). Brain activity and growth go hand in hand. It is not only a question of 'use it or lose it' says Susan Greenfield (1997: 115), but 'use it as much as you can'.

In the first three years of life, the neural connections are established at a phenomenal rate. By the age of 5 or so, they begin to tail off and are virtually complete by age 10 (Gammage 1999). However, this does not mean that after age 3 no worthwhile learning can take place, or that if connections are not made by age 3 then an individual has lost the opportunity for development and growth. Some writers, in their eagerness to exhort the benefits of early learning, have suggested that if a child has not been fully stimulated by age 3 then their opportunities for learning and development become closed off. Mercifully for most of us, this is not the case! The brain may not 'grow' more neurons, but it does go on making connections and these can be stimulated at any age (Bruer 1999). However, it does seem that there are critical periods in development where experience has significant effects on brain functioning. In other words, the best time to master a skill associated with a system is when a new system is coming on line in the brain (Sylwester 1995; Pinker 1997; Bruer 1999). Language is a good example. It is easy for a 2- or 3-year-old to learn any language, but if that person waits until age 18 or 30, learning a new language will be more difficult because the systems governing this process may have been used for something else. However, not all critical periods happen in the first three years, nor do all cognitive systems show such effects (Bruer 1999). As educators, it is important that we do not make claims for early learning that are overly expansive. Nonetheless, a realization of the critical importance of brain connections to human growth and development should challenge educators to ensure that the learning environments that are created and the support that adults give to young children as they learn, maximizes their drive to make as many connections as they can with what they already know and understand.

What do young children learn?

Given an appropriate environment in which they thrive, what is it that young children are learning? Shaffer claims that 'we change in response to the environments in which we live' (1993: 5). The change is particularly in response to the actions and reactions of the people around us. We behave in new ways because of our observations of and interactions with important people in our lives and are affected by the events we experience. Young children come to make sense of their world by observing, imitating, investigating and exploring. They learn attitudes, skills, strategies and concepts that enable them to understand and be understood.

Positive *attitudes* to learning arise from children's motivation to learn, to succeed in the face of many odds, and to master the exciting and intriguing world around them. The posing of personal problems teaches children the value of concentration and perseverance in the successful acquisition and honing of skills and understandings. Success fuels their motivation and determination to succeed and enhances their confidence and self-esteem as learners. The infinite range of new and exciting things to discover and explore stimulates young children's curiosity and engages their eagerness to be both successful and competent.

Important *skills* are learned as a result of establishing patterns of behaviour which ultimately become automatic. Young children repeat movements or actions time after time in order to become expert and succeed at the goals which they have set themselves. Skills usually develop in the course of activities that the child sees as being worthwhile and which give him or her the motivation to continue, sometimes through failure after failure, to succeed. Children are motivated by the response of others, particularly their parent or carer, and this response sustains them through the frustrations of learning to stand alone, throw a ball towards someone else or make their desire for food clearly understood.

In the course of learning skills, children develop their own peculiar set of *strategies* for trying out, rehearsing or repeating what they have done. Some children prefer to look and think before they act. Some try and try again until something comes right. Some prefer to imitate, some to instigate. Some ask questions and others wait for answers. Whatever strategies are developed, they are tailor-made by each child. They are chosen because they serve the child's individual purpose and because they work. These strategies become part of the characteristics of the child as a learner and are the basis of all strategies that will be adopted if the child is left to learn alone.

The understandings or *concepts* that children learn are generally arrived at through a process of abstraction of the principles that underpin a number of different experiences. Children come to understand about size, colour, the past or the seasons through a variety of first-hand experiences, leading them to see and understand the conceptual links between one experience and another. In this way children become able to generalize abstract principles from concrete experiences. It is almost impossible to rush this transition from concrete to abstract because if children are forced to establish connections then it is likely that they will make inappropriate ones (Brierley 1994; Robinson and Beck 2000).

We know that children *do* make the wrong 'connections' and that, once made, these misunderstandings – or alternative understandings – can take a great deal of unlearning. The work of Wynne Harlen, Roger Osborne and others reveals that children have views about a variety of topics and that they are very often different from the views of 'experts'. However, to children they remain 'sensible, useful views' (Harlen 1985: 76) and can remain uninfluenced or be influenced in unanticipated ways by teaching. The views that children hold are a result of their personal endeavours to construct their own meaning for, and understanding of, the experiences they have had (Postlethwaite 1993). They work for the child who has constructed them and since they serve the child's purpose reasonably well, they may not readily be displaced by the explanation of someone else especially, as Postlethwaite says, as these explanations are often more complex than their own.

Readiness for learning

Inherent in beliefs about the competences of young children is an attitude towards the concept of 'readiness' for learning. If children are viewed as competent young learners, then it follows that they have predispositions to learn from their earliest days and, as such, are ready for learning from birth (and, some would say, before). The consequence of this view is that children are never *not* ready to learn and the notion of children 'emerging' into literacy (Hall 1987), numeracy (Hughes 1986) and so on, assumes engagement in concepts which at one time would have been deemed inappropriate for young minds. The work of Donaldson (1978), Bruner (1986), Hughes (1986) and others, however, has encouraged the view that children are ready for learning if learning is adapted to the intellectual proclivities of children (Watson 1998).

Once again we are drawn to the behaviours of parents and carers who appear to make these adaptations instinctively. Parents, it seems, adapt naturally to their child's intellectual tendencies, attributing consciousness and intentionality to their child's actions from the very beginning of his or her life (Stern 1985). When parents talk to their child they do so as if expecting a response, often long before the child seems capable of giving one. In this way, suggests Watson, children's early learning is aided in spontaneous and incidental ways by older and more experienced members of their community, who give structure to the child's earliest, hesitant inclinations to explore the world (1998).

A child is ready to learn when their cognitive disposition and what is to be taught are matched. Parents may make this match instinctively knowing, as they do, so much about the body of beliefs, expectations and assumptions that their child brings to a learning situation. Teachers do not have the benefit of sharing each child's learning history and one of the most complex challenges of teaching is to become as knowledgeable as possible about the cognitive dispositions of a large number of children in any one class.

Much of the influence of Jean Piaget stemmed from his view that children progress through various stages of development that determine their current level of skills and competence. Readiness for learning, he believed, depended on the child's developmental stage, and progress from one stage to the next could not be rushed. This view of development influenced many teachers to adopt a relatively passive role in children's progress (Darling 1994). Teachers planned activities that reflected the notion of readiness with titles such as 'pre-reading', 'pre-number' and so on. The role of the teacher was to bring children to a state of readiness to engage fully in significant skills or concepts and children were taken through a whole range of early stages of learning in preparation for their arrival at the next stage of development. Piaget's notion of readiness was ultimately challenged by a number of researchers, noticeably Margaret Donaldson (1978), who believed that children should be actively encouraged to move towards the 'disembedded' thinking that characterizes learning in schools. The work of Lev Vygotsky (1978) has also been highly influential in this debate about readiness. Vygotsky believed that instead of matching teaching to existing development, teaching had to proceed in advance of development in order to challenge and extend children's maturing functions. He believed that learning comes in advance of development when progress is stimulated and guided by the expertise of others. This notion of readiness places the emphasis not so much on *when* to teach, but rather *how* and *what* to teach.

The characteristics of successful early learning

Young children may be inexperienced learners, but their competence should no longer be underestimated. Modern technology has made it possible to investigate the very beginnings of human thinking, and researchers have documented critical development in the pre- and postnatal months of life (Carnegie Corporation 1994). From the beginning, humans demonstrate intention-directed behaviour (Blenkin and Kelly 1987). They are both intellectually and interpersonally engaged, or predisposed to be so, much earlier than previous theories allowed (Watson 1998). The young child is clearly emerging cognitively, linguistically, physically, socially and emotionally and – most significantly – this critical development occurs when the child is receiving no formal education. Children have the capacity to draw conclusions about the world when the knowledge that they need has not been formally taught to them.

Given an environment in which they are cared for and in which they can thrive, young children display a range of competences that make their early learning dramatically successful.

- Young children display positive *attitudes* and *dispositions* to learn. The determination for mastery over their environment drives them to persist and persevere – often in the face of difficulty and initial failure – to succeed in their objectives.
- Young children develop personal *skills* and *strategies* that work for them in their quest to understand the world. These strategies are chosen instinctively and fulfil children's purposes for the particular task in hand.
- Young children have developed *understandings* and sometimes *misunderstandings*. Each piece of knowledge acquired, each small piece of sense that is made, fits into each child's personal cognitive jigsaw.

The construction of this personal cognitive jigsaw has many parallels with the construction of the traditional wooden puzzle. At first, the pieces of cognitive jigsaw are picked seemingly at random. Sometimes the piece fits straight away, sometimes it is turned round and round – with astonishing patience – before the fit is finally made. Sometimes the piece is turned round and round and a fit is made and only subsequent pieces show that piece to be in the wrong place. Sometimes the piece is turned round and round, does not quite fit but is jammed in anyway because it is more satisfying to have reached a solution than to have to start again.

It is the skill of the educator to be aware of the pieces of the jigsaw that the child already has in place and whether or not they have been fitted together correctly. If they have not, then supporting the child to review the construction of their cognitive jigsaw is as delicate and difficult an operation as persuading the child to select an alternative piece of wooden puzzle. The 'teacher' – whether an adult or another child – needs to be informative without being imposing. Imposition simply leads to the learner becoming confused and disaffected. Confusion arises because the links between the pieces have been made by the teacher and not by the learner. Disaffection occurs because the initiative has been taken away from the learner and the construction no longer makes personal sense.

The expertise of the child's first educators

We have seen that young children's early learning is not only the result of their own predispositions to learning, but also the result of interactions with significant others in their family and their community at large. It is important to appreciate the strategies that parents use which make them such successful educators, very often without realizing it.

- Crucially, of course, most parents *love* and *care* about their children and have a genuine interest in their actions, ideas and development. Parents may be very busy, be feeling under the weather, be preoccupied with other things – but the bond between them and their children surfaces under all manner of stresses and strains to reassure the child of the strength of the relationship between them (Sylva and Lunt 1982).
- Parents *operate in the real world*. They talk to their children in kitchens and bathrooms, they take them to shops and playgrounds and cinemas, they eat with them in front of the television or in McDonald's. Parents and their children are

surrounded by a cacophony of visual, aural and tactile stimuli – sights and sounds that constantly fascinate children and cause them to ask what, how and why?

- Usually, parents give children *time* to learn; time to pose meaningful questions and to come up with their own theories and hypotheses; time to try things out, to make mistakes and to try again; time to leave things be, to return to them at will and to revisit things when the time is right; time to be distracted and to take a detour from their original path or goal and to learn by accident rather than design.
- Very often, parents are in a *one-to-one situation* – or at least one and a very small group situation – when these questions are asked. Although every parent knows that feeling of being asked one question too many, research into the interactions between children and their parents and children and their teachers (Tizard and Hughes 1984; Wells 1986) reveals that however brief, not to say curt, parental responses might be, that parents still interact far more frequently with their children than the teacher with their 10, 20 or 30 children. In the home, children are able to talk about a range of topics, to initiate and sustain conversations and to ask questions endlessly, and all of these factors make the home 'a powerful learning environment' (Tizard and Hughes 1984).
- In these situations, parents usually *respond to*, rather than *initiate* learning. The child wants to know, wants to know what to do, wants to know what to do next – and the parent is there to supply the appropriate piece of the jigsaw, there to support and to facilitate the developing learner.

Studying children and their parents can offer those of us in formal education many lessons about effective early learning. It is so important that teachers draw on the expertise of parents and enable them to inform us and to go on informing the school about their child. It can be too easy to pay lip service to the notion of a partnership with parents, but teachers should not forget that it is *they* who join the already established learning partnership that exists between the parent and their child.

How do young children learn?

While it is possible to identify the learning characteristics of young children, it is altogether more difficult to try and understand exactly how they learn. There is no conclusive evidence on this subject, although there have been a number of influential theories over the course of the last two centuries. The theories have grown and developed one from the other and many have, at some point or another, had an impact on the way in which children have been educated (see Entwhistle 1987; Wood 1988; Anning 1991).

Young children learn by being active

Any personal study of young children reveals almost non-stop activity in the quest for skills, strategies and understandings. The work of Jean Piaget and other contemporary theorists of child development emphasizes that 'being active' does not necessarily mean 'moving around', however. Being active means that the young child *engages* with experiences, actively (as opposed to passively) bringing his or her existing knowledge and understanding to bear on what is currently under investigation. Being active is what causes children both physically and cognitively to construct their own view of the world, to personalize the experience and to apply it in ways that make sense to them as individuals (Bruner and Haste 1987).

Young children learn by organizing their own learning experiences

The work of Chris Athey at the Froebel Institute has provided a new framework for studying the patterns of children's behaviour as they learn. These early patterns of behaviour (or schemas, as they are defined) are seen in babies, and become more complex and more numerous as the child develops. By becoming familiar with these behaviours, the observer realizes that actions are not performed in isolation but are one of a set of experiences coordinated by the child (Nutbrown 1994). Athey, in her book *Extending Thought in Young Children* (1990), illustrates how such patterns can be represented in children's play, their thinking and their language. Once in tune with these categories of behaviour, adults have a valuable framework for observing children's actions. Schemas are a way of understanding the learning behaviours of children and, as such, give adults and educators an appreciation of what is currently interesting and absorbing the child. 'It is through schemas, and the fitting of content to different schematic threads, that children's own construction of reality and sub-sequent continuity can be identified' (Nutbrown 1994: 36).

Young children learn by using language

The language development of young children is a staggering phenomenon. The increase in young children's vocabulary and their growing capacity to use language for a range of purposes is powerful evidence of an innate drive to make meaning and to communicate. The research of Gordon Wells and his team on the Bristol Language Study concluded that in the early stages children's linguistic systems are more or less in place and a basic vocabulary of several thousand words is acquired. From that point on, however, what is learned and the order in which it is learned becomes 'progressively more dependent on experience – on having opportunities to hear the relevant functions, meanings, and structure used appropriately and to use them oneself' (Wells 1986: 32).

Wells sees language as a code to be cracked, but that before the child attempts this, he or she has already become familiar with the code in use. Language development relies on children hearing and using language in meaningful interactions. In order to work out for themselves how language is organized, children need the collaborative help of 'conversational partners' who 'provide clear and relevant feedback', enabling children to evaluate the appropriateness of their current hypotheses. This does not mean that it is necessarily best for adults to overtly teach children the use of language. As in other areas of their development, children construct their own internal models of language and rather than adults teaching children, says Wells (1986: 48), 'it is children who teach adults how to talk in such a way as to make it easy for them to learn'.

Language provides not only a means of acting on the world, but also for reflecting on that action in an attempt to understand it (Harlen 1985). Piaget argued that language is a *medium*, a method of representation within which thought takes place. Vygotsky, on the other hand, believed that speech transforms the way in which children learn, think and understand and is, therefore, a *tool* of thought (Wood 1988). The theories of Jerome Bruner draw and build on the work of both Piaget and Vygotsky. His assertion is that the internalization of language is an instrument of thought and that the very young child uses language 'almost as an extension of pointing'. All of these theories depend on the understanding that thought, action and language are inextricably bound together in children's development. The successful development of all three is dependent on experiences being embedded in what is meaningful for the child.

Young children learn by interacting with others

Children may well be active learners in a highly individualistic sense, but they construct their personal meanings within the framework of a social and cultural context (Wood 1988). The young child is a social being, playing, talking and living alongside others, watching what they do and imitating them, questioning what is seen and responding to questioning, drawing on the knowledge and expertise of others to interpret and make meaning of experiences (Richards and Light 1986; Wells 1986; Dunn 1988). Everything that young children learn is influenced by the culture in which they grow up and the community in which they live. The writing of Vygotsky emphasized the significance of social contexts for learning, whereby adults – or other more expert members of the community – help children to acquire skills and understandings that they might not accomplish, or accomplish less speedily, alone. Vygotsky refers to the gap between what children are able to do alone and what they can achieve with help, as the 'zone of proximal development'; in other words:

> the distance between the actual developmental level as determined by independent problem solving and the level of potential development as determined through problem solving under adult guidance or in collaboration with more capable peers.
>
> (Vygotsky 1978: 86)

The work of Wood *et al.* (1976) extends this notion, adopting the metaphor 'scaffolding' to describe the guidance and interactional support given by the adult or expert until the child is able to take over tasks for themselves. In this model of learning, children are not passively absorbing the strategies of the adult, but take an active, inventive role (Smith 1993), reconstructing the tasks through their own understanding while the adult or educator provides what Bruner (1985) describes as a 'vicarious form of consciousness'.

Implications for classroom practice

What then are the implications for classroom practice of the issues which this chapter has raised? What strategies do teachers need to consider if they are to build on what is known about how young children learn?

Young children learn by being active

If young children learn naturally by being active and engaging in a range of exploratory experiences then the primary responsibility of the school is to plan opportunities that facilitate and support these instinctive strategies. Children need opportunities to engage with a range of materials and stimuli. They need time and space to explore, investigate and question. They need a range of play experiences and appropriate resources of good quality. They need, in other words, a learning environment that offers concrete experiences that are relevant, meaningful and worthy of active involvement. If children are to continue their struggle to make sense of the world, then the world must be worth the struggle. Clearly, before children start school, the incentive and motivation to learn have been sufficient. It is up to schools to make children's new learning environment equally worthwhile. Some teachers have been concerned that supporting this development demands the construction of individual learning programmes. Although the development of each child is unique, however, there are also similarities between how children in general develop and therefore many ways in which teachers can and should plan for children's learning as part of a small or larger group (see Chapter 6).

The introduction of the literacy and numeracy strategies in England seriously undermined some of the active and dynamic learning experiences that teachers normally planned for their children. The initial emphasis on the elements of – particularly – the literacy *hour* (as opposed to the *strategy*) caused many early years practitioners to feel pressurized into making children sit for long periods of time and to learn literacy and language skills in a very decontextualized way. Mercifully, as teachers, headteachers, consultants and advisers have become more confident, the rigidity of the hour is giving way to the more flexible use of the many valuable features of the strategies in more learner-friendly contexts. Early years teachers need reassurance that what they know about the idiosyncratic learning styles of young children should always take precedence over a one-size fits all framework for the teaching of such key skills.

Young children learn by organizing their own learning experiences

Athey (1990) reminds us that in order to tap into the personal constructs of the child, teachers need to focus on the underlying processes of their thinking and cognition. When teachers are concerned with the sense which children are making of their own learning then this provides a rich source for planning and development. Observation and appreciation of children's schemas can offer teachers a starting point for planning experiences that capture children's current interests and absorptions. If a child is focusing on a trajectory schema – a fascination with things moving or flying through the air (see Bartholomew and Bruce 1993 for further definitions of schema) – then 'he or she needs to be provided with a range of interesting and stimulating experiences which extend thinking along that particular path' (Nutbrown 1994: 15). When children are absorbed by something in this way, it is far more productive for teachers to go with and plan for that interest. Starting from the child becomes increasingly difficult when there is an external curriculum to be taught (Chapter 3 will address this issue in depth), however, teachers who believe in working with rather than against the interests of children will make time to observe and record the ways in which they organize their own learning experiences. Nutbrown says that those who become interested in children's schema development come to know that children will pursue their schemas, whether adults like it or not!

Young children learn by using language

The work of Margaret Donaldson demonstrates the importance of young children's experiences being embedded in contexts that are meaningful to them (1978). Her work, and that of researchers studying the relationship between language development in the home and at school, emphasizes the importance of the contexts in which the adult and the child have shared experiences in common from which to draw shared meanings (Anning 1991). Edwards and Mercer (1987) claim that the establishment of mutual understanding and shared meanings is something with which teachers also must be concerned. They suggest that of the points at which education commonly fails, is when 'incorrect assumptions are made about shared knowledge, meaning and interpretations' (1987: 60). Teachers and pupils need to share a 'common knowledge' about the discourse that forms the basis for classroom communication in order for the learning that comes from interaction to be most effective.

Children use language to learn and therefore classrooms must give them opportunities to use language in a variety of ways. It is language that affords young children the means of making sense of their experiences and of internalizing their actions. In order to capitalize on the power of language to influence both thought and action, classroom experiences must encourage talk as a key process through which young children learn. It is heartening to find a renewed emphasis on speaking and listening in the new Early Learning Goals and the *Curriculum Guidance for the Foundation Stage* (QCA/DfEE 2000) and that the Parliamentary Under-Secretary of State for Education and Employment at the time of writing acknowledges listening and speaking as two of the 'key learning skills' of the Foundation Stage (QCA/DfEE 2000: 2). Talking something through, either alone or with others, is an important way of grasping new ideas, understanding concepts or clarifying feelings and perceptions. Young children need opportunities for discussion, for explanation, for description, for narration and for speculation. In classrooms where talk is recognized as a powerful and natural medium for learning, young children are able to make meaning of what is new in terms of what is familiar. Through their talk, they create for what is new a context that is personal to them and one that relates to their own experiences (Britton 1970).

Young children learn by interacting with others

If learning is socially constructed then teachers clearly have a critical role in classrooms, a role at one time devalued by misunderstandings about the nature of 'child-centredness' and 'discovery learning' (Blenkin and Kelly 1987). It is the skilled intervention of the teacher which will move children from their present to their future potential. Interactions with children must facilitate this progress through Vygotsky's 'zone of proximal development' and teachers must arrange things, says Athey (1990), so that knowledge is actively constructed and not simply copied. Teachers need to plan classroom time so that they have regular conversations with children. These conversations need to be designed to find out what children already know and understand (see Chapter 2) or to support, through questioning or answering questions, the child's current thinking. Such conversations need to be planned and not to happen incidentally. To bring this about, teaching time needs organization, so that adults can focus on their planned learning objectives and not be distracted by unrelated interruptions.

Other children are also part of this social construct, and teachers have to look at 'the context in which learning takes place in schools as well as at the nature of specific learning tasks' (Pollard and Tann 1993). The topic of children working together and learning together is discussed fully in Chapter 6, but there is growing evidence of the importance of peer tutoring in classroom contexts – whether teachers plan for it or not (see for example Forman and Cazden 1985). Effective teaching acknowledges the role of *all* those who have knowledge and understandings to contribute to the development of individual learners.

Conclusion

When children start at school they are already competent learners. Competence has evolved from the fusion of the child's natural predisposition to learn and the appropriateness of the support he or she has received while learning. This chapter suggests that those responsible for the more formal stages of children's education need to look to the characteristics of children's successful early learning environments in order to develop models of teaching that will lead to the continuation of effective learning throughout the child's school life. In the following chapter we examine how teachers establish the range of competences that children bring to school and how teachers come to find out what children already know about and can do.

2

CONVERSATIONS AND OBSERVATIONS

Establishing a baseline

Introduction

If we acknowledge that children bring to school certain skills, knowledge and understandings then a key task of the teacher is to identify precisely what it is that children already know and can do in order to build on their existing competences. This immediately defines the classroom experiences of both teachers and children. If children already know and can do a range of things, then it puts the teacher in the role of learner alongside their class. The teacher must find out the extent of children's competences to ensure that the planned curriculum is appropriate to this particular class and its individual members. This leads to planning that is tailor-made for each child because the foundations for learning are unique. Each child has his or her own personal history of experiences, which will determine not only what they need to learn next, but how they will do so most effectively.

Establishing the starting points for children's educational experiences is not a task that takes place only when a child begins school. Teachers need to establish the starting points for children's learning throughout their schooling as part of the ongoing cycle of teaching and learning. All too often the planned curriculum establishes its starting points from what has been taught in school, and what a previous teacher has 'covered'. However children continue to learn in and from a range of contexts that are nothing to do with the classroom, and it is always necessary to discover what knowledge and understanding children bring with them from their previous life experiences in order to plan a curriculum that matches their current learning needs.

The teacher as learner

Placing themselves in the role of learner, teachers make assessments of children's knowledge, skills and understandings before finalizing the planning of an appropriate curriculum. All too often, assessment is seen as the end of the teaching process, undertaken to discover whether children have learnt what was planned. There is, however, a critical place for assessment at the start of the cycle of teaching and learning, when teachers find out what children already know and can do so that the next experiences planned are relevant and meaningful. This process should happen not just when children start school but at the beginning of each fresh teaching cycle. Assessment is a tool that begins and ends successful teaching. At the beginning it establishes what is currently known and at the end it establishes what has been learnt as the result of the planned curriculum. This chapter is concerned with the two key ways in which teachers establish, at the beginning of the teaching and learning cycle, what children already know and can do. The first strategy is to have *conversations* with those who know about the child as a learner. The second strategy is to make *observations* of the child in action as a learner.

Having conversations

Teachers need to have informative conversations with a range of people who have knowledge of the child as a learner. These conversations need to inform the teacher about:

- what interests the child;
- what motivates the child to learn;
- how the child perceives him or herself as a learner;
- what the child already knows about and can do;
- what the child would like to know about or do.

Having a range of conversations gives teachers a range of perspectives on each child and these perspectives help to form a rounded and balanced picture of the child. Each perspective is valid and needs to be valued, and each contributes something fresh to the teacher's understanding of the child and their needs. Putting together this profile is rather like undertaking a detective investigation as the teacher gathers together the pieces of the evidence that they need in order to make hypotheses and judgements upon which to proceed in their work.

Conversations with children

Conversations with children – where children do most of the talking – provide teachers with evidence of children's responses to learning and to experiences. They offer the children's version of what they have just experienced – not the *intended* learning outcomes, but the *actual* learning outcomes. They reveal how children have approached an activity, what they found interesting, what strategies they used for making sense of the world and where any misunderstandings might be. Such conversations give teachers hard evidence of children's development. When children have to put into words what they have done and learnt, and how they have gone about it, then their thoughts and language give us clear evidence on which to build the next stages of learning. At this age, oral evidence provides more detailed and reliable information than recorded evidence. The capacity of young children to think and understand far outstrips their capacity to interpret that knowledge and understanding in recorded form and written evidence can present a very limited version of their experiences. The very act of articulating ideas and understandings reveals a wealth of information about the child's learning: what they have understood, what they have misunderstood, what skills they have used and what they have enjoyed. Conversations with children offer the teacher a marvellous assessment opportunity as they reveal needs *and* interests, and can be a critical moment in the cycle of teaching and learning.

It is crucial that conversations are meaningful to the child and that the teacher genuinely wants to find out about what he or she is asking about. Questions should demand answers that the teacher does not already know, otherwise the questioning technique is simply being used as a checking device, to discover whether children are paying attention or not. Young children are all too aware of whether teachers' questions are genuine. This is scathingly exemplified by 5-year-old Sonnyboy who responded to his teacher's meaningless questioning with a question of his own: 'Why do you keep asking the kids questions when you knows all the answers? Like . . . like . . . what colour is it then? You can see for yourself it's red . . . so why do you keep asking them?' (Cousins 1990: 30).

Skilful, open-ended questioning leads children to share their own thoughts, ideas and perceptions with the teacher and teaches the teacher something more about the child. When young children record what they know or understand then the evidence of their learning may be far more limited. It can be limited by a child's capacity to record, to write or draw what they have done or understood. It can be limited by the child's understanding of the task or the worksheet. It can be limited by the page or sheet that simply requires that boxes are filled in and leaves no space for the child's original thought or interpretation. Since schools have been subjected to inspection by the Office for Standards in Education (Ofsted) there has been great concern amongst early years practitioners that evidence of children's achievements must be in written form. It is often believed that a child's picture, model or talk does not carry the same weight as a piece of writing, and worksheets are more and more in evidence. This is very misguided. A child is far more complex a learner than can ever be evidenced by a worksheet. If we want to have evidence of what a child knows and understands then we must collect the richest and most powerful evidence available – the child's own actions and the child's own words.

Conversation with parents

Conversations with parents and with carers add to the developing picture of the child as a learner. Parents bring their knowledge of the child in a variety of contexts which the teacher may never be privileged to see. A good case for home visiting is made when teachers recount what they have learnt from seeing the child in the surroundings of their own home, and how relationships change when parents meet teachers on their own territory (see Edwards and Redfern 1988, for a very practical account of the development of partnerships with parents).

Conversations with parents should take place before the child starts school, when the child starts school and after the child has started school. The conversations need to acknowledge the expertise that parents have about their own children and the understanding that parents have about their children's needs and interests. If teachers want to know about children in order to build on the children's existing abilities, then part of that knowledge comes from parents, and teachers need to acknowledge this by providing a range of opportunities to listen to and record parental knowledge, attitudes and ideas. These conversations should happen just at the beginning of the child's school or class experience. Parents continue to have a fresh, different and crucial perspective on their child's development, their attitude to school and learning and their growing skills and competences. We all know that children can behave as two different beings – both in attitude and approach – from home to school, and it is an impoverished profile of the child as a learner which only takes account of the child in the context of school.

> It would not make sense to try to educate a child without taking account of the most significant people in his/her environment, and trying to work with them. It is through the home context that school becomes meaningful, or not, to a family.
>
> (Bruce 1991: 15)

Much of the following material about parental partnership is taken from the Oxfordshire Education Department *Curriculum Matters* series on Early Years (1996). It looks, in practical ways, at strategies for developing effective relationships with parents and carers.

Before children start school

From the time a family first makes contact with a school, or a school first makes contact with a family, there are opportunities for a dynamic partnership to be established. To enable this to develop, schools could offer some of the following:

- an invitation to use the toy library and/or book library;
- invitations to school events such as assembly, performances, fairs and other special occasions;
- invitations to share amenities such as a wild area, hall, family room or swimming pool.

These informal contacts are invaluable for building confidence between parents, children and the school staff. From such beginnings a more formal induction process can evolve naturally.

Parental entitlement

Each school needs to think carefully about how they help *all* parents and children to feel valued and welcomed at the beginning of their school life. Teachers may want to consider the extent to which, in their school, parents have an entitlement to:

- share their greater knowledge of their child, prior to entry, and throughout their time in school;
- enter a partnership with the school which takes account of various cultures, languages and styles;
- sufficient time and opportunity for regular formal and informal communication with the school;
- dialogue with teachers where parents' opinions and ideas are valued and have influence;
- communicate their aspirations for their children;
- comment on and contribute to the records of their child's achievements in all areas of development.

Parental partnership

In order to facilitate a partnership with parents, schools may need to initiate many or all of the following strategies:

- visit families at home (remembering that some parents may prefer to meet in school);
- design an entry profile for completion by parents and children;
- use photographs and/or a video camera to record everyday and special events;
- communicate school aims and routines using visual material;
- share school activities by making a range of small books;
- use home/school diaries, either audiotaped or written (community languages should be used where possible);
- organize a range of times during the day and evening for meetings and appointments;
- organize a crèche for younger children;
- arrange for someone at meetings who can speak the community languages;
- enable an outreach worker/key worker/friend to attend with a family if support is required;
- adopt a flexible and imaginative response to the needs of families and the community;

- respect the variety and depth of information that parents convey about their children;
- recognize the diversity of values within the wider school community;
- give parents opportunities to express their own expectations of the school;
- give parents opportunities to express their hopes for their children both inside and apart from school;
- give parents opportunities to express their own fears and misgivings;
- ask parents to describe:
  their child's interests,
  what their child can do,
  their child's health,
  what is special to the child,
  what the child hopes to do at school,
  their child's likes and dislikes,
  the history of their child's experiences,
  their child's friends,
  people who are important to the child,
  what the child fears about school;
- share the strengths and achievements of the child at school;
- discuss ways in which parents and the school can work together to support the child's learning.

Conversations with parents can benefit all parties concerned. It benefits teachers because of their increased knowledge of the child, it benefits parents by making them genuine partners in their child's learning and it benefits children, who see home and school as mutually interested in their education.

Conversations with other adults

The third group of people with whom the teacher needs to have conversations is those other adults who have experience of the child as a learner outside the context of the home and before starting school. Playgroup leaders, childminders or private nursery providers may all have worked with the child in a very different context than the home. They will have experience of the child in settings that require social adjustments and institutional expectations. These practitioners will have experience of the child in varied learning situations and will have much to contribute to the picture of the child as a learner.

The 1997 UK government requirement to establish an Early Years Development and Childcare Partnership in each local authority has brought together practitioners from a range of agencies concerned with the education and care of young children. Teachers, health visitors, playgroup supervisors, social services daycare workers and a range of others now plan collaboratively and cooperatively to improve the quantity and the quality of provision for young children in their local area. These more formal interagency structures have encouraged a fresh dialogue between professionals who have similar concerns for and about children's growth and development. They have also opened up a more steady flow of information about what each agency does, the principles it holds and its specific aims and objectives. The Early Years Development and Childcare Partnerships have made a highly valuable contribution to more 'joined-up thinking' on the part of early years practitioners, as well as local authority officers and elected members.

Two other government initiatives have drawn attention to the growing need for practitioners in different sectors to work together and form closer informal partnerships. The first was the introduction in 1998 of national baseline assessment. Although the 'measurement of children's attainment [to be] used for later value-added analyses of children's progress' (SCAA 1997: 2) is carried out in the first seven weeks of a child's entry to primary school (either the reception class or Year 1), a requirement for the accreditation of all local authority schemes was that scheme providers must include guidance on procedures for 'how teachers can use records of children's pre-school experience, where these are available, to inform the assessment of their attainment and to help plan for their further learning' (SCAA 1997: 6). This presented local authorities with the challenge first of finding out whether primary schools *did* receive records from preschool settings and, second, whether they were valuable to reception and Year 1 teachers in making their baseline assessment judgements. In local authorities where there is a mixed economy of maintained, independent, private and voluntary sector early years provision, this was a particular challenge. Some primary schools receive children from as many as 10 or 12 preschool settings and the quantity and quality of preschool records vary considerably. However, this has given practitioners an incentive to devise a system that would be manageable and appropriate for all settings, and would give reception and Year 1 teachers greater consistency in the information they received. (There is a more detailed examination of baseline assessment in Chapter 10.)

The development of local baseline assessment schemes was perhaps the first real challenge to practitioners to address the issue of continuity and progression in young children's early educational experiences. Providers across all sectors began to talk together and work together in new and productive ways, and many barriers began to come down as people shared their experiences and their practice. In Oxfordshire, the Early Years Team introduced paired training sessions, where the allocation of places was conditional upon the attendance of a practitioner from the primary school *along with* a practitioner from one of their feeder preschools. By receiving training together, relationships are forged and understanding greatly enhanced. This paired training initiative has proved very popular and has been extended to cover other key aspects of early education such as play and the outdoor curriculum.

The introduction of the Foundation Stage for learning (QCA/ DfEE 2000) for children age 3 to the end of the reception year has already had a significant impact on the issue of continuity and progression. The establishing of this distinct phase of education has highlighted for many people just how disparate and disjointed children's early experiences are during this crucial phase of their development. At a time when they need to be so secure and form stable relationships with key adults (Rutter 1995; Elfer 1996), young children are often faced with some of the most dislocated experiences of their lives. It is not unusual in the UK, for a 3-year-old to go from home in the morning to a childminder, from the childminder to a half-time nursery, from the nursery to a playgroup, from the playgroup to the childminder and from the childminder back home, *and this is all in one day*. What does this reveal about the value that the UK has placed on the social and emotional needs of such vulnerable individuals? It is outrageous that such young children are subjected to this amount of upheaval and change, and shows only too clearly why a national early education and childcare strategy in the UK is so desperately needed. Until the government establishes a coherent system for high quality education and care for the whole of the Foundation Stage experience, in one setting, with well-qualified adults who are familiar to the children, then it is imperative that early years practitioners increasingly work together to make young children's experiences more seamless. The most precious commodity for everyone is time. If children's experiences are to be assessed and planned in a cohesive way, then practitioners need time to visit each other and to talk to those to whom they send and will receive Foundation Stage children.

Making observations

The other key mechanism for finding out what children already know and can do is through observations of them while they are in action as learners. Children are naturally active learners (Bruce 1987; EYCG 1992), so it is imperative that to learn about them teachers should watch them in action. If our objective is to find out the full range of what children know and understand then this cannot be achieved by limiting the observations that are made. Children should be observed while they are engaged in a range of activities, both teacher-initiated and child-initiated, which should occur:

- in familiar learning contexts;
- in an environment that encourages confidence and builds self-esteem;
- alongside a range of peers;
- when a child is working with an adult;
- when the child is working independently;
- at different times of the day and week.

Teacher-initiated and child-initiated activity

Observations of children need to encompass activities that have been self-initiated and those that have been initiated by the teacher. Self-initiated activity gives children opportunities to make choices and decisions of their own. It enables children to demonstrate their independence as well as their social skills in choosing to work with others. Self-initiated activity gives children control over situations, and sometimes their peers, and puts children in rare positions of classroom power (Warham 1993). Appropriately resourced and supported, child-initiated activity can bring about some of the most creative and innovative learning in the classroom (Whitehead 1993).

Teacher-initiated activity is equally important. A key purpose of education is to broaden the range of children's knowledge

---

Box 2.1   Example 1: Building a balanced profile

A student on teaching practice was building a very thorough profile of a 6-year-old boy in her class and was using it to try and establish why his behaviour was antagonistic and why she had such difficulty in engaging and sustaining his interest. When we looked at the profile together it became clear that she had made observations of the child when engaged in activities which *she* had initiated. Although she was aware that he 'liked making things' she had no observations of his involvement in self-selected tasks from which she might make judgements about future, more appropriate, planning. For the next few days she observed the child engaged in self-initiated activities and soon found that he did indeed enjoy making things, particularly with construction kits, and was very skilful at it. Talking with him about his models she found that he was very knowledgeable about aeroplanes and regularly visited air shows with his father. When working on his self-selected tasks, she was amazed to see that he was cooperative and supportive to other children who worked alongside him. The student learnt that there was another side to this child. She saw a side of him that, observing him in directed situations, she might never have seen. By combining her knowledge of the child in both situations she was able to plan teacher-initiated tasks which incorporated the positive aspects she had learnt about the child through her observations of his self-selected activity.

---

and experience and this is appropriately planned for by the specialist practitioner. In teacher-initiated activities there are opportunities for children to work with a variety of adults and peers for a range of purposes. Children engage in ideas and actions that are new to them and which they may not have discovered for themselves.

Both kinds of experience – teacher-initiated and child-initiated – are important and one without the other will not give children sufficiently broad and balanced opportunities for learning. Equally, one without the other will not give the teacher a sufficiently rounded picture of the child as a learner. Box 2.1 illustrates the importance of knowing as much about the young learner as possible.

Familiar learning contexts

If teachers are to observe children and have conversations with them in contexts in which they will be at their best, then it seems advisable to establish an environment that is familiar and which builds on the best of children's preschool experiences. We have already seen in Chapter 1 how successful a child's first learning environment is. As well as the home situation, however, many children have other valuable preschool experiences that can give an insight into the kind of educational environment that will stimulate and involve them as learners. The ways in which children of 3 and 4 years learn so successfully does not dramatically change with the blowing out of five candles! The introduction of the Foundation Stage should encourage all providers of early education to develop provision and practice in line with the excellent aims and principles set out in the *Curriculum Guidance for the Foundation Stage* (QCA/DfEE 2000). As the quality of education across different sectors improves, children should not have such a disparate experience as they move into primary school. Nevertheless, I still believe that provision for the Foundation Stage will not be totally adequate until children receive that educational experience in the same high-quality setting from age 3 to the end of the reception year. Only in this way will planning and provision be as continuous, cohesive and comprehensive as it needs to be and only then will the needs of children and families be met effectively. The Early Excellence Centres and Sure Start initiatives have provided first-class models of integrated services to meet the needs of young children and their families. The government's funding of nursery schools throughout England since 2001 is supporting the development of these specialist settings in similar, innovative ways. The time is ripe for some radical rethinking about how early education and care in England is planned and managed.

An environment that encourages confidence and builds self-esteem

Confidence and self-esteem are built in a myriad of ways and many of these have already been mentioned in this chapter. Children's self-image is enhanced when their culture and traditions are respected and acknowledged by the teacher and used in the planning of an appropriate curriculum. Young children's feelings and attitudes are crucial to their achievements in all aspects of life and this has been recognized in the Early Learning Goals and the *Curriculum Guidance for the Foundation Stage* (QCA/DfEE 2000). It is important that those of us working in the field of early childhood education fight to preserve the affective elements of the curriculum and to sustain the social and emotional aspects of children's development. Rosemary Roberts (1995a) has examined how children's feelings affect their attitudes to school and shows how self-esteem can be the key to effective teaching and learning. As teachers we can help to build self-esteem through the response that we give to children and to their attitudes, ideas and efforts. This does not mean heaping them with empty praise but supporting them in the self-assessment of their achievements and encouraging them in the development of their abilities (see Box 2.2).

To have positive self-esteem children need self-confidence and this can be powerfully developed when children are encouraged to use their initiative, to make decisions and to be responsible for sharing in the planning and the evaluation of their work. If we want children to develop positive self-esteem then we have to show them that they are capable, however young they are, of decisions that have an impact on their own experiences and their own lives. Children who are proud of their cultural heritage, their gender, their family and themselves have been profoundly affected by the attitudes of those around them and the teacher is a critical part of that network of influence (Siraj-Blatchford 1994). If we are to make observations of children that reflect the best that they can do, and in which they have the confidence to share with us what they know, then we must give them an environment that encourages their confidence and builds their self-esteem.

A range of peers

As early years practitioners, we are rightly concerned with the social development of children. As with all other aspects of their development, the social experiences of children before they start at school will vary enormously. Some may have come from large, extended family groups, including brothers, sisters, uncles, aunts and grandparents. Some may have had significant periods of time with childminders or at playgroup or nursery and have become used to working and playing alongside their peers. For

---

Box 2.2   Example 2: Responding to children's work

A teacher of a vertically grouped class of Year 1 and Year 2 children wanted to develop the children's ability to evaluate their own work. She wanted them to move away from relying on her for decisions about whether what they had done was 'enough' or 'good enough'. She suspected that this reliance stemmed from the fact that, as she had set the tasks, the children believed that only she could judge the quality of the results. So she decided to change the entire way in which she introduced activities to the class. After the initial discussion and the introduction of the activity she would ask the children what they thought was important in completing the task. She supported the children in thinking through the processes, the skills, the knowledge and the understandings they might need to demonstrate in the course of the activity and what the outcomes might be. They then decided which of these were the most important and these were recorded on a large sheet of paper and left pinned to the wall. At the end of the session the children would gather with their work and then review their own efforts against the criteria, which the class had collectively compiled. In this way the children were developing their personal responses to their own work and in the process were being challenged to use their initiative and to take responsibility for their learning and its outcomes. The teacher reported growing confidence and self-esteem as the children became involved in setting their own criteria for achievement in this way.

---

some children, however, school will be their first introduction to the competition, collaboration and cooperation that is required when you are one amongst a number of others, all vying for space, resources and attention. Like all skills, being sociable is something you get better at with practice. The more people you meet, the more you learn to adjust and adapt to differences in attitudes and behaviour. Some people are better at this than others; some children are better at this than others. Home circumstances, life experiences and general dispositions will mean that certain children are ready to work in a range of social situations while others need support to increase their social skills. The more opportunities children have to work alongside the full range of children in the class, the more opportunities they will have to learn those social skills that will make school life, and life in general, a more positive and pleasurable experience. If young children are grouped early, in fixed groups, they may miss out on many of these valuable social experiences (see Chapter 6). Children should be able to communicate and cooperate with a range of others irrespective of their gender, race, physical attributes or ability. A profile of the social development of the child is best founded on observations of children working alongside a range of peers, demonstrating a whole range of characteristics, attitudes and personalities.

Children working with an adult

There will be many opportunities for teachers and other adults to observe children while they are working alongside them. By supporting a child in a task, or facilitating their activity, the adult is able to observe and, if appropriate, to record what the child says and what the child does as evidence of their growing conceptual awareness or skill development. They can also observe *how* the child approaches tasks, what strategies they use for solving problems, their persistence and motivation and their attitudes in general. What has to be remembered is that the presence of the adult will, to a lesser or greater degree, alter the behaviour of the child; to what extent depends on the task and also on the sensitivity of the adult. If a child is engaged in an adult-initiated activity and that adult is close by, then the child may frequently look to the adult for affirmation that they are doing the task 'right'. Some research in a reception class (Fisher 1996) illustrated the impact of the task on children's reliance on the teacher (see Box 2.3).

When a teacher gives a child a task and then sits with them while they tackle it, then the child's approach and the amount of support they look for will have a significant impact on the process and probably the outcome of the task. This is not to say that a teacher should not work alongside a child – far from it. The teacher's role in supporting, challenging, guiding and extending children's learning is critical (see Chapters 1 and 4), but it is important to be sensitive to the impact the presence of

---

Box 2.3 Example 3: Building independence

As a researcher, I spent one day a week for two years in the same reception class, observing the interactions throughout the day between the teacher and members of her class. There was very clear evidence that the more directed the task, the more frequently the child went to the teacher for help and, particularly, affirmation. As the teacher's aim was to make the children more independent and to give herself more time to focus on her planned activities, this observation presented her with an instant strategy for achieving both aims at once. If she wanted to be less interrupted, and have time to work with particular children or do an observation, then the rest of the class had to be engaged in tasks which were less prescriptive and over which they had more control. The teacher changed the balance in the activities she planned. The activities where there was an adult present were more directed and the activities where children were working independently were more open-ended. Once this new way of planning was established, the teacher reported far fewer interruptions by children engaged in independent activities.

---

a teacher, or any adult, can have on the process and outcome of any activity.

Children working independently

When children work independently, they display different behaviours and often different strategies and skills than when they work under the direction of an adult. Dependent upon how much independence they are used to in their classroom generally, an observation of children working alone usually reveals fresh perspectives on the children as learners. Children's responses will be affected by whether the task is self-chosen or initiated by the teacher, whether they have been told to collaborate or whether they have chosen to do so, and whether or not there is a required end product. Whatever the task, the conversations of children working independently usually reveal far more about children as learners than is revealed when they work on tasks where adults are present.

Different times of the day

Until relatively recently, it was common practice in many infant classes that children worked in the morning and played in the afternoon. Apart from the fact that this is pedagogically flawed (see Chapter 3) it also works against all that is known about human physiology. Children are no different from adults; some are 'larks' and some are 'owls' – those who wake up bright and perky and irritatingly cheerfully straight away, and those who begin sluggishly, but improve as the day goes on. Observation of children at different times in the day shows us that some children take a long time to settle in the morning, while others can concentrate almost immediately. There are some children who are adversely affected by breaks in the school day – assembly, television and so on – whereas others seem to take these in their stride. Many children are affected by playtimes and lunchtimes and take a long time to settle afterwards. My reception class research showed that it can be the period from break to lunchtime that is the most disrupted. After lunchtime, children were tired but usually more able to settle to their various tasks than after break when they were still wound up from rushing around, and needed more intervention from adults to engage in their activities (Fisher 1996). Because children are human, they will be at their best at different times in the day, so it is important that when we observe them we take this into account, and do not always observe at the same time of day, and do not always assume that all children will be at their best at nine in the morning.

The introduction of the literacy and numeracy strategies have seen an unwelcome return, in some schools, to a timetable based on similarly ill-conceived notions. These schools have adopted a timetable where literacy takes place across all classes until breaktime followed by numeracy from breaktime to lunch (or the other way round). All other aspects of the curriculum are subsequently squashed into afternoon sessions and all reports on current curriculum provision show that the teaching of art and design, physical education, science, information and communication technology (ICT) and the humanities are being squeezed into smaller and smaller amounts of time. For the youngest children, some of whom attend only part-time, this diet has not been modified. Consequently these children are receiving only literacy and numeracy education, frequently in a form that is inappropriate for their age and stage of development. Not only that, but these literacy and numeracy experiences are disembedded from those meaningful experiences found in more integrated learning environments. The impact of creative and physical skills and experience on children's capacity to develop number concepts and literacy are well documented (see for example Edwards and Knight 1994; EYCG 1998) and it is an impoverished curriculum that offers these two crucial aspects of education in such a disembedded way. The introduction of the Foundation Stage should ensure that children, up to the beginning of Year 1 at least, have a more broadly-based and rounded curriculum experience, but there needs to be greater understanding on the part of many managers and governors, that young children's experiences often need to be different and distinct from those that are appropriate for children who are older. It may look neat and tidy if all curriculum planning, records of assessment and timetables are uniform from reception to Year 6, but it will *not* necessarily meet the learning needs of children.

The purpose of observations and conversations

Teachers who want to find out about children choose strategies that tell them the most. Unless those strategies leave room for the teacher to learn from the process, then the strategies will not be informative but merely affirmative. Teachers come to know what they already know and teaching remains rooted in *assumptions* about what children need to know next.

Having made an observation or recorded important elements of a conversation, the teacher needs to translate these records into appropriate action. The professional skill of the teacher is in knowing what it is that they have seen or heard in relation to each child's development. They have to make decisions about whether what they have seen or heard means that something particular needs to be planned and whether the individual has needs that have not previously been identified. Much of what has already been planned will remain relevant, but ongoing assessments of children inform the fine tuning of short-term plans (see Chapter 3) and enable teachers to ensure that time is spent on a curriculum that starts from the needs and interests of the child.

Conclusion

Having conversations with children and observing them in action acknowledges the competences with which children come to school, not only at the beginning but throughout their school careers. Observations and conversations are tools for assessment that recognize children's individual competences as the baseline against which their future learning needs should be identified. Such assessment practices define the role of the teacher as being that of a learner, alongside their class, finding out about and then building on what children already know and can do. The assessment practices described in this chapter are the starting point for planning rather than the finishing point. The next chapter explores how teachers use the information gained through initial assessments of children to plan an appropriate curriculum.

3

PLANNING FOR LEARNING

Decisions about an appropriate curriculum

Introduction

Acknowledging the child as a competent learner should ensure that the starting point for planning an appropriate curriculum is the child's developing skills and understandings. These competences are established through the initial assessments of children described in the previous chapter. What children already know and can do should determine the experiences that are planned for their development (Bruce 1987; DES 1990; EYCG 1992; Ball 1994.) However, the imposition of an externally imposed National Curriculum and the introduction of first the Desirable Learning Outcomes (DfEE/QCA 1998) and now the Early Learning Goals (QCA/DfEE 2000) challenged the plausibility of such a notion. Many practitioners have felt torn between their early years principles, rooted in the ideals of child-centredness, and their statutory obligations to meet an agenda purporting to meet the needs of all children rather than those of the individual learner.

There is now, at times, a perceptible tension between the interests of young children as learners and the interests of their educators. Early years educators, like all of the teaching profession, have goals to reach, targets to meet and standards to raise. These are the outcomes by which they are inspected and against which they will be judged. Although the most recent early years curriculum guidance (QCA/DfEE 2000) attempts to be more learner-centred, the external agenda inevitably puts pressure on teachers to cover the curriculum rather than allow children, in Lilian Katz's words, to *uncover* it (Katz 1998). There is a pervading concern amongst practitioners that to detour from the planned path, to encourage children to divert or digress, will mean that outcomes will not be achieved and that somehow this equates to failure. It is a real dilemma that the standards agenda, so beloved of recent UK governments, has attainment as a marker of progress. High attainment has always been easy if you narrow the range of things that are to be attained. Look how many children in the 1960s and 1970s got to the top of the reading scheme – but could not transfer any universal reading skills to other texts. However, the Foundation Stage has been wisely and aptly named. Foundations have to go broad and deep before a building can go high. If the foundations of learning are to be adequate, then it may be some time before the building is actually seen. Once constructed, however, the building should go higher and be more adaptable than anything constructed with narrower, more hurried, less secure foundations (Fisher 2000).

The notion of child-centredness

Early childhood education is rooted in a belief that children should receive an education designed to meet their own indi- vidual needs. Child-centred thinking has its roots in the work of philosophers such as Rousseau and Dewey and stemmed, as described by John Darling (1994) in his review of child-centred education, 'from radical dissatisfaction with traditional practice'. This practice was characterized by an emphasis on content over process and on the memorizing of facts rather than an under- standing of concepts. Classes were taught as a single entity, with little or no account taken of individual differences in previous experiences, current understandings or rates of progress. The time- honoured metaphor that children were 'empty vessels to be filled' made the classroom roles of children and teachers very explicit. It was the duty of teachers to fill the vessels with knowledge and the duty of children to learn what was being taught, and if they did not, then the onus of blame was well and truly on *their* shoulders.

Yet long before such practice was established, there was a commitment to the notion of children as individual learners. As early as 1762, Jean-Jaques Rousseau declared in *Emile* that 'Nature provides for the child's growth in her own fashion, and this should never be thwarted' (Rousseau [1762] 1976). His approach to thinking about children and their development was taken forward by such writers as Pestalozzi, Froebel and Dewey, each developing and revising the work of the others until a powerful philosophy for the education of young children was formed. However, it was not until the 1960s that this philosophy really began to have any impact on practice in Britain. The main reason for the change in pedagogy was the public endorsement of a more child-friendly approach by official reports, most noticeably *Children and their Primary Schools* (The Plowden Report; CACE 1967). The Plowden Report heralded a more liberal view of education, encapsulated in the celebrated quotation:

> at the heart of the education process lies the child. No advances in policy, no acquisitions of new equipment have their desired effect unless they are in harmony with the nature of the child, unless they are fundamentally acceptable to him [*sic*].
>
> (CACE 1967: para. 9)

Child-centred education is concerned with the *development* of children. It is seen as a natural progression that is best aided by adults who, in Darling's words, 'have an appreciation of and respect for the ways of children' (1994: 3). This is an important element. Part of the criticism of child-centred practices was that the child was able to choose and control their own actions and that the role of the teacher diminished for fear of being accused of 'interfering' with this natural development (see Blenkin and Kelly 1987; Darling 1994).

Interestingly, it was the work of Jean Piaget (1896–1980) that did much to fuel this misconception. Piaget believed that children pass through certain stages of development and could not operate at the later stages before passing, in their own good time, through the earlier ones. This theory supposed that children passed through these stages irrespective of adult support and that the best an adult could do was interfere! The obvious assumption was that if children passed naturally through these stages of development, then the most dangerous thing one could do was to rush them through the process.

This theory led to the notion of 'readiness' (see Chapter 1), with teachers believing that they had to *wait* until a child was ready to learn something rather than being in a position to move them on or extend them beyond the stage where they were. Such a notion rendered the teacher somewhat impotent.

Knowing the next stage of development and perceiving the learning needs of the child are of restricted use if you believe that it is damaging to use such knowledge. The other facet of Piaget's work which apparently diminished the role of the teacher was his emphasis on the child as an individual explorer of the world, discovering and making sense of new situations through action and self-directed problem-solving (Bruner and Haste 1987). Piaget's influence on thinking and practice in the 1960s and 1970s caused many practitioners, as well as critics, to believe that the role of the teacher had been sidelined and that children were to be encouraged to do as they please. The power of these assumptions can be seen all too clearly in the series of Black Papers written between 1969 and 1977 (see Cox and Dyson 1969a, 1969b, 1970; Cox and Boyson 1975, 1977) and the impact of the resultant conservative backlash is, I would suggest, still being felt today.

Much of Piaget's work became challenged even by those who acknowledged his tremendous contribution to the development of our thinking about children and their learning. One of the most influential challenges came from his colleague Margaret Donaldson. In her book *Children's Minds* (1978) she argued for a fresh interpretation of Piaget's views based on her own research in which she replicated some of Piaget's tests but using significantly different methodology. She and her colleagues found that by setting Piaget's tasks in contexts that were familiar to the children and using language that was clear and relevant to the tasks, a significantly greater number of children were able to complete the tasks than had succeeded in Piaget's original tests (Piaget and Inhelder 1956). Donaldson's work adds powerful weight to the notion of the young child as a competent learner and the critical role of the teacher in extending those competences:

> the normal child comes to school with well-established skills as a thinker. But his [*sic*] thinking is directed outwards on to the real, meaningful, shifting, distracting world. What is going to be required for success in our educational system is that he should learn to turn language and thought in upon themselves. He must be able to direct his own thought processes in a thoughtful manner. He must become able not just to talk but to choose what he will say, not just to interpret but to weigh interpretations. His conceptual system must

expand in the direction of increasing ability to represent itself. He must become capable of manipulating symbols.

(Donaldson 1978: 88–9)

As was described in Chapter 1, Lev Vygotsky (1896–1934) offers a very different view of the role of the teacher. Vygotsky saw children's cognitive development operating at two levels, the present level and the potential level. He believed that the role of more knowledgeable others is to move the child from the actual to the potential next level of understanding. The task of the teacher is to encourage children to do *without* help what they can do only at present *with* help (Anning 1991). In other words, children's learning can be extended by the right intervention at the right time.

Teachers have a highly interactive role in a Vygotskian framework. Children's development is static unless they are able to work in their zone of proximal development. Teaching does not wait upon development but propels it.

(Smith 1993: 56)

This support for children's learning is what Wood *et al.* (1976) have called 'scaffolding', and this offers an appropriate metaphor for the notion of child-centredness in its aim to plan activities, resources and interactions that match the level of competence and maturity of the child. The work of Jerome Bruner (1915–) is of particular relevance to early years practitioners because he works from an analysis of children's learning, to a model of classroom pedagogy and then to a curriculum framework. It is the very fact that the National Curriculum attainment targets and the Early Learning Goals work in precisely the opposite way that seems to set them at odds with the notion of child-centredness.

Comparisons between the pioneers and modern theorists

The child-centred notions of Rousseau, Dewey, Pestalozzi and others can be seen clearly in the principles and practice of the early childhood educators such as Froebel, Montessori and Steiner. Tina Bruce's book *Early Childhood Education* (1987) takes the threads of influence even further by comparing the principles of those early pioneers with the work of more modern theorists such as Piaget, Vygotsky, Bruner and Mia Kelmer Pringle, founding director of the UK National Children's Bureau. The 'ten common principles of the pioneers' (Bruce 1987) is a valuable framework for the development of good early years practice in current settings. These principles have been adopted and developed in many subsequent documents (e.g. EYCG 1992; Roberts 1995b). The Oxfordshire Early Years Team (1996) have adapted them to reflect their work with children 0–8 years, and the adaptation in Box 3.1 offers indicators of those early years principles in practice.

Box 3.1   Principles of early childhood education

1   *Childhood is seen as valid in itself. It is a stage of life and not simply a preparation for the future.*

- experiences and environment should be appropriate to the age and developmental stage of the child;
- experiences should be relevant to the child's *current* needs;
- each child should be valued for themselves, what they are, what they know and what they can do;
- learning at this stage may improve later performance but, first and foremost, learning enables children to achieve their present potential and enriches and fulfils their present life (Moss and Penn 1996).

2   *The whole child is considered to be important; social, physical, intellectual, moral and spiritual aspects of development are related.*

- all aspects of the child should be considered in planning provision and experiences;
- the balance between these areas needs to be sustained once children begin statutory schooling;
- *all* areas of development should be observed and assessed in order to inform future planning.

3   *There is potential in all children which will emerge powerfully under favourable conditions. Each child is unique and special, with individual ways of learning.*

- every child should be known well by at least one adult;
- children should be valued with full regard to their gender, race and ability;
- the environment should be sufficiently flexible and responsive to meet the range of children's learning styles and strategies;
- children need time and space to produce work of quality and depth (EYCG 1992).

4 *Parents are the first and continuing educators of their children. Schools should value and build on parental expertise.*

- schools need to establish systems where parents can tell the school about their child;
- schools should develop a partnership with parents and carers based on mutual respect and a shared interest in the child;
- parents should be involved in the process of assessment and contribute to decisions about future plans for their child.

5 *Learning is holistic and interconnected. The young child does not separate experiences into different compartments.*

- short-term planning should be sufficiently flexible to make space/allow time for the children's spontaneous interests;
- planning should identify the understanding, skills and attitudes that are important for developing learners; activities and topics should support rather than determine these objectives;
- broadly based and integrated experiences are appropriate when working within the National Curriculum.

6 *Young children learn through exploration, play and talk.*

- young children learn most effectively by doing rather than being told (EYCG 1992);
- play should occur throughout the day, alongside teacher-directed activity;
- play is given status when it is valued, assessed and used to extend learning;
- children should be encouraged to initiate conversations and pose questions.

7 *Our starting points for supporting learning are what children* ***can do*** *and what they* ***can nearly do.***

- children should be helped to identify their own targets and achievements;
- observation-based assessment should be the basis for planning;
- adults should sensitively support and extend children's learning.

8 *Intrinsic motivation is recognized and valued as a powerful force for learning.*

- autonomy (physical, social and intellectual) and self-discipline are emphasized;
- children should have periods of time for sustained self-initiated activity;
- children should have the opportunity to make choices and decisions.

9 *The relationships that children establish with adults and other children are of central importance in their development.*

- the education of young children should be the responsibility of appropriately trained and experienced educators with a knowledge of child development;
- children need planned experiences that encourage the interpersonal and cognitive skills necessary for collaboration and cooperation;
- teachers should be aware of themselves as models.

10 *Children's education is seen as the total experience of, and interaction with, their environment.*

- children's schooling should draw on their personal context of family, culture and community;
- there should be provision and planning for an indoor and outdoor environment of equal quality;
- the way in which we talk and respond to children throughout their time in school should create a climate that nurtures self-esteem.

The translation of principles into practice has been particularly influenced by the writing of Geva Blenkin, who espouses a commitment to a developmental view of education and argues cogently for a concept of education:

> not as a device for the transmission of certain bodies of agreed knowledge and values or as a process of moulding people into some predetermined shape, it is of the enhancement of capacities, the widening of every person's horizons of appreciation and understanding, the maximization of everyone's potential, the development of everyone's powers of self-direction, autonomy, understanding and critical awareness.
>
> (Blenkin and Kelly 1987: 11)

In Chapter 2 of *The National Curriculum and Early Learning*, Blenkin, in Blenkin and Kelly (1994: 29) draws together four broad themes of early childhood education which, based on the principles of a developmental curriculum, are peculiar to that stage of education:

1 The young child is dependent on adults and is new to institutional life. The process of learning to be a pupil is thus of great importance.
2 Rates of development and learning are at their most rapid during this stage of education, and they are highly susceptible to environmental constraints and advantages. The young child, therefore, needs to be stimulated by a wide range of experiences rather than confined to a narrow and restrictive programme.
3 Although social interaction is important at every stage of learning, it is of particular importance at this early stage, since young learners are not able to make sense of experiences which are represented in a more formal or abstract way.
4 Early education must not only provide a rich array of practical experiences but it must also nurture the playfulness of children. For secure mastery of skills or knowledge depends on play, because it is through play that the child is able to test out, informally and personally, what is newly learnt.

As early years practitioners, we are challenged to plan a curriculum that:

- focuses on process rather than content or outcomes (or targets or goals);

- offers a wide range of experiences rather than a restrictive one (or imposed one);
- emphasizes first hand, real experiences that contextualize learning (rather than a diet of workbooks or worksheets);
- emphasizes active learning and play (rather than passive learning and pencil and paper activities).

It would seem that the fundamental tenants of good early years practice fly in the face of the National Curriculum, national literacy and numeracy strategies and Foundation Stage goals, which often fail to recognize 'what a complex and subtle matter is the learning of pupils in their early, formative years' (Blenkin and Kelly 1994: 197).

The *Curriculum Guidance for the Foundation Stage* (QCA/DfEE 2000) at least has aims and principles that reflect good early years practice and do nothing but support the place of active learning, play, first-hand experience and process as key elements of effective provision. Nevertheless, while there are goals to be reached, early years practitioners will always have to guard against pushing children to fulfil the school's agenda of reaching them, rather than responding to the pace or direction that is in the best interests of the individual child.

The National Curriculum and early learning

Blenkin and Kelly's critique of the National Curriculum outlines certain key features which they believe render it wholly inappropriate as a curriculum framework for young children. First of all, it does not take account of the intellectual needs of young children or see them as being qualitatively different from those of older pupils. Second, it ignores the 'manifest advantages of play' and the merits of a holistic approach to the curriculum. Third, the National Curriculum does not acknowledge that young children need assistance to structure their own knowledge and make sense of their own worlds. Fourth, it takes a limited and simplistic view of what the teaching and learning of subjects entails in the early years. Fifth, it has no research base of its own and manifestly ignores the accumulating research evidence for appropriate high quality early years education (see Sylva 1994). Finally, what is happening in England and Wales contrasts starkly with policy developments in almost every other country in the world.

Much of this criticism has seen a response in the introduction of the Foundation Stage principles and its accompanying curriculum guidance. Young children's learning has now been recognized as qualitatively different from that of older pupils. Children aged 3, 4 and 5 are acknowledged to deepen their understanding by 'playing, talking, observing, planning, questioning, experimenting, testing, repeating, reflecting and responding to adults and to each other' (QCA/DfEE 2000: 6). Older learners learn effectively this way too of course, but the curriculum guidance is a refreshing antidote to the rigidity of some aspects of other relatively recent government documentation. I am full of admiration for those teachers who have resisted the pressure to reintroduce word tins for the 40 high frequency words; give worksheets to teach isolated, decontextualized phonics; destroy wonderful texts by relentless references to print, comprehension, sentence construction and punctuation and keep children on the carpet come what may until the prescribed 30 minutes has passed. The national literacy strategy may not have intended to stifle young children's literacy and language development but in many cases the overrigid implementation of the literacy hour has. Thankfully teachers – and headteachers – are becoming increasingly flexible in their application of the literacy and numeracy strategies and are using their content in ways that are more recognizable as good early years practice, 'with opportunities for all children to explore, enjoy, learn about and use words and text in a broad range of contexts' (QCA/DfEE 2000: 8).

Subject knowledge

The pressure to demonstrate subject expertise has had a significant impact on initial teacher education, and two issues in particular have affected courses for students wishing to teach in the early years. First, it has been deemed desirable that primary teachers – including those who want to specialize in the age range 3–5 years – have been required to have knowledge of subject application for Key Stage 2 children as well as early years and Key Stage 1. This has resulted in time for students to learn about how young children develop and how they learn being significantly reduced and, in some cases, eliminated altogether. Teachers of young children need to know how children develop just as much, if not more, than how subjects develop, however. The Rumbold

Report *Starting with Quality* (DES 1990) stated unequivocally that 'For the early years educator . . . the process of education – *how* children are encouraged to learn – is as important as, and insepar- able from, the content – *what* they learn' (para. 68). It is a lack of understanding of young children's learning processes and the impact these have on their educational development, that char- acterizes current policy decisions. If children's learning were uni- form and their responses mechanical, then a curriculum that focused on 'delivery' would be not only appropriate but effective. It is the idiosyncratic nature of learning, however, that makes teaching so demanding and so rewarding. How dull it would be if all children learned in the same way, with the same motiva- tion, at the same rate and with the same result. If we begin to train generations of teachers who do not know what to do when children respond in unexpected ways then the blame will revert to the child. Teachers need to look reflectively at their own practice and make adaptations and adjustments in order to teach all children effectively.

There is little disagreement amongst educationalists that in teaching, an understanding of the major disciplines and the means for making these accessible to young children is essential (Aubrey 1994). The world of school has been shown by Donaldson (1978) and Tizard and Hughes (1984) to be discontinuous with the rest of the child's world, however. The *application* of subject knowledge and expertise is most successful when students and teachers learn about how children learn and develop so, as Aubrey suggests, they can apply the subject in contextually appropriate ways and the generalized mass of subject matter can be taught effectively to a range of children with a range of learning needs. Calderhead and Miller (1985) suggest that teachers interweave knowledge of subjects with a knowledge of classroom realities to create 'action-relevant' knowledge – the kind of knowledge that you *really* need when faced with a class of 30 interested and lively 5-, 6- or 7-year-olds.

Although every child (and indeed every adult) brings a unique set of experiences and understandings to each learning situation, it is possible – and as far as the teacher is concerned essential – to see that there are also generalizable patterns in children's development. Unless teachers of young children acknowledge and articulate these patterns, they are faced with an insurmountable task in planning and implementing a curriculum that fosters learning in a class of up to 40 children. As Angela Anning (1991) stresses, it is important to retain insights into the particularities of each child as a learner and to respect their individuality, but it is equally important to acknowledge their similarities.

Similarities and differences between young learners

When considering similarities and differences, I believe that it is helpful to reflect on the need for different approaches between teaching and assessment. When making assessments, children *must* be seen as individuals. The teacher is looking for what the individual knows, understands and can do. Having made these assessments which are concerned with the individual, however, it will then be seen that certain children have similar needs as well as having those that are different. Teaching can thus be planned to meet either the similarities or the differences. On many occasions a group or class can be taught something in the same way at the same time. However, there will be some children for whom a certain stage, approach or concept is wholly inappropriate and in order to meet their particular needs something different has to be planned.

While I do believe that there are tensions between the National Curriculum and a developmentally appropriate early years curriculum (see Blenkin and Kelly 1987) and between the Early Learning Goals and notions of learner-centred education, I also believe that there are ways of looking at the apparent dichotomies which may make the application of one not wholly incompatible with the constraints of the other (see for example, EYCG 1998). I think that some of the answer to easing the tension lies within a better definition of the major stages of curriculum planning. Schools and teachers have been increasingly required to plan in depth at each stage – long, medium and short term. Definitions of these stages have been prolific and sometimes conflicting. While not wishing to add to the plethora of definitions, I would suggest that the answer to this fundamental early years dilemma is to see long-term and medium-term planning as meeting one set of needs and short-term planning as meeting a different set. Long-term and medium-term planning are about the curriculum and about subjects. Short-term planning is about the child. If we can make and sustain this differential then it may be possible to sustain a developmental position while meeting the requirements of the external agenda.

Stages of planning

Long-term planning is concerned with children's entitlement to a *broad and balanced* curriculum and is achieved through the appropriate allocation of time to the teaching and assessment of the Foundation Stage curriculum, the National Curriculum, religious education and other curriculum aspects identified by the setting.

Medium-term planning addresses *continuity and progression* from one stage in each area of learning/subject to the next, and from one setting or class, drawing on schemes of work and the long-term plan and identifying the concepts, skills, knowledge and attitudes to which children will be introduced over a specified time. It is at this stage that the curriculum may be most effectively organized by linking together different areas of learning/subjects through themes or topics. However, medium-term planning should also record the ongoing learning that will take place alongside any planned topic work.

Short-term planning is concerned with *differentiation* and planning for the needs of specific classes, groups and individual children. It provides the detail of activities, experiences, resources, groupings, adult support and teaching strategies which are identified through ongoing observation and assessment of children in action.

Long-term planning

Long-term planning usually takes place well before the start of the new school year. In many schools this stage of planning is formalized in planning cycles that identify the precise areas of learning to be addressed by each class, every term. Such planning, while it may attribute to overall school effectiveness (Ofsted 1994a), cannot purport to be concerned with the developmental needs of individual children because teachers have frequently not yet met their class, indeed some children will not yet have started school! Even if the classes are known, the children's needs will have developed way beyond any planning that can be identified for them some 12 or more months prior to the teaching. Some practitioners will already be wanting to argue that a developmental curriculum should not seek to constrain the learning of a young child by even suggesting, this far in advance, what they will experience. Perhaps this is where the compromise comes in. While a curriculum is in place to which all teachers must adhere, there seems little point in offering solutions which are immediately unworkable. Long-term planning is about children's entitlement to the curriculum and most practitioners will be comfortable with a framework that is chiefly concerned with the breadth and balance of children's experiences during their time in the setting.

Medium-term planning

It is at the medium-term planning stage that I feel most difficulties lie. Medium-term plans are usually written at the start of a new term or half-term, or at the beginning of a theme or topic for younger children. Although the children may now be known to the class teacher, their developmental needs are not. Children's needs change rapidly at this stage in their development – too rapidly to be predicted, with accuracy, several weeks in advance. So it is important that medium-term planning also addresses subjects and areas of learning, rather than children. The most important feature of medium-term planning is that it should identify the concepts, skills, knowledge and attitudes that are the intended learning outcomes for that period of time. It may also show how these are to be integrated and linked together into themes or topics. However, all too often, on carefully produced planning sheets, there is a column for the activity or task which will be the vehicle for the intended learning outcomes. If a decision is made that this activity or that task will be appropriate for a child before their actual needs are known, then the decision may be the wrong one. There is a lot of sense in pencilling in possible activities and accumulating a bank of ideas from which to draw, but activities are only the vehicles for learning and planning must be sufficiently flexible to change activities and to accommodate the needs and interests of individual children, once they are known.

Topic work

Topic work acknowledges the fact that children do not naturally compartmentalize their learning into subject areas. It seeks to capitalize on the notion of cross-curricular learning, with its intention of mirroring the real life learning of children in a range of contexts. However, I feel there is a danger that cross-curricular learning and topic work are no longer the same thing. Cross-curricular learning emphasizes the opportunities for children to cross the boundaries between traditional subjects and see the application of skills and the consolidation of concepts in experiences and activities that enable such cross-fertilization to occur. Topic work, while rooted in this notion, has been hijacked by teachers and their agenda. Increasingly as topics become planned by whole staffs together, the links that are made between areas of learning are not seen by the child but engineered by teachers. They sometimes involve excruciating contortions to involve all areas of learning and the links are at times quite incomprehensible even to a trained adult who knows the game that is being played. We must guard against making topics as incomprehensible to children as subject divisions are.

A further concern for early years teachers is the expectation that they fit in with the school cycle of topics. Very often the topic titles are inappropriate for young children and do not meet their current needs and interests. Equally, topics and themes may not last as long for younger children as they do for older pupils and yet early years teachers feel locked into the cycle and compelled to continue with a topic even when it is not bringing about effective learning. Either way, teachers in the early years should have the flexibility to select topics for the length of time they are relevant and meaningful to the children. Topics should be as expendable and exchangeable as activities. They are the vehicles for learning, not the purpose of it. If one topic, theme or activity better suits one class or group than another, and either can bring about the intended learning, then any planning system should be sufficiently flexible to accommodate the changes.

Short-term planning

It is at this stage that planning moves from concerns with the curriculum and subjects to concerns for the child. It is at this stage that the teacher has the opportunity to incorporate the developmental approach to learning, by making first-hand observations of children engaged in active learning and through having conversations with children about what they have experienced. Through observation of children in action, carrying out open-ended tasks that allow them to explore and investigate, teachers can gain information about children's knowledge and understanding as well as their skills and strategies. All of this information is necessary if teachers are to plan a curriculum that has relevance and purpose for each child. The intention or objectives of the activity will come from the medium-term plans, but the actual activity, task or experience will be planned in the light of what the child already knows and can do, and what the teacher judges he or she needs to know or do next.

Assessment activities

It is at this stage that it would be helpful to look again at the cycle of teaching, assessment and learning that determines the activities which teachers plan for children. As we saw in Chapter 2, assessment activities are often seen as a check against the effectiveness of teaching, a measure of whether children have learnt what it was intended that they should learn. As such, assessment frequently comes at the end of the process and often gets tagged on to the seemingly more important stages of planning and teaching. I would suggest that this model of the cycle is limited and very often ineffectual. If assessment is only ever seen as completing the cycle, however, then the use of assessment to inform future planning may be highly restricted. It leaves teachers either predicting or guessing what knowledge or understanding children bring to the introduction of a new concept or the learning of a new skill. Teachers often make elaborate introductions to new ideas and then use the discussion time following the introduction to elicit a range of understandings from children. However, this knowledge is not always used to inform or to alter planning. If teachers always begin by teaching, then there is an implicit assumption that what has been planned is appropriate and that, apart from the necessity for differentiated follow-up, the needs of children will be met.

We have seen, however, that children bring with them to school a whole range of knowledge, understanding and skills which are nothing to do with the formal education of school. Peers, different adults, the television, books, outings and visits all give children a vast array of insights which teachers ignore at their peril. It is inappropriate to introduce the concept of magnets to a child whose father is a scientist who has conducted experiments with his young son since the age of 3 (see Box 3.2). This is a trap that is easy to fall into but can just as easily be avoided.

Box 3.2 Example 4: What William already knew and understood

William stayed at the magnet table for 12 minutes. In that time he did not pick up a single magnet. He became absorbed in the workings of an egg whisk – one of the items that had been left for the investigation. He turned the handle this way and that, watching the blades rotate. He held the whisk up-side down and sideways. He tried to engage another child in this investigation, but the boy was too busy discovering for himself that 'you can make it stick through paper . . . look!'. William persevered until, having exhausted his investigations, he looked for the teacher and went over to show her what he had discovered. As a result of this she was able to plan for him to use a construction kit that enabled him to make his own 'blades' using cogs and wheels. The child was the son of a scientist. He didn't need to explore the properties of magnets, he knew about them.

By setting up this experience, the teacher not only reminded herself of William's knowledge and understanding in this area – and, to varying levels, that of three other children in the class – but she was able to offer William something to meet his particular and highly specialized needs. As I have already said, when making assessments of children we will not find that every single child needs something different every single time. In this instance William needed something highly specific. The three other children with experience of magnets needed some-thing else, and the remaining children all needed similar experi-ences because they were new to magnets and their properties and needed time to come to understand the concept of mag-netism through further investigation and exploration.

A very valuable part of the planning process should be the designing of activities in order to assess what children already know and can do (see Chapter 2). In other words they come before the *new* skills, concepts or knowledge are introduced in order to ascertain precisely the starting points of each child's current knowledge and understanding. The tasks need to be as open ended as possible and children should have a variety of opportunities to explore, experiment, investigate and hypoth-esize, giving the teacher every indication of what is already known and understood. Such activities need to encourage children to take risks so there can be no right answers and no predicted outcomes. So, for example, if a teacher's medium-term planning identifies the introduction of using the senses to explore and recognize similarities and differences between materials, the assessment activity might involve leaving on a table a variety of magnets and a variety of objects that attract or repel the mag-nets. The teacher then observes from a distance how different children approach the investigation of these resources and listens to the conversations they have with each other in order to learn what they already know and understand. Box 3.2 is an observation made of William, aged 4 years 10 months, in the classroom.

There are many occasions when assessment should *begin* the cycle of teaching and learning and teachers' plans should remain flexible until precise knowledge of the children is gained. There is always a danger that when involved in long- and medium-term planning, teachers draw on records from previous teachers/year groups and if an area or subject has not been covered in a previous class then the assumption is made that an individual child knows nothing about it. All the children then receive the same starting point or complete scheme of work according to the *presumed* lack of knowledge. As professional educators we must make it our business to find out what individual children already know and can do and ensure that our planning builds on this knowledge.

Differentiation

While long- and medium-term plans are the concern of the staff as a whole and may well be similar in format, short-term planning should be more responsive to the requirements of individual teachers. Teachers need to adopt strategies that allow for these short-term plans to address the issue of *differentiation*. Differentia-tion is the key to matching experiences to the developmental needs of children.

Most reports on the quality of primary education have con-firmed that the quality of learning experiences is related to the degree of match between any planned task and a child's previous experiences and current educational needs. Research into classroom practice (Galton *et al.* 1980; Bennett *et al.* 1984) and government-generated reports (Ofsted 1991, 1993a, 1994b) suggest that this match is frequently not achieved. It would appear that teachers often direct the level of planning towards children of average ability, with the consequent underestimation of high attainers and the overestimation of low attainers.

There are undoubtedly many reasons why this situation exists. First, there has been an overload of curriculum content and assessment practices (Campbell *et al.* 1993). Second, some teachers' classroom management strategies do not allow for observations to be made on which they base effective, detailed assessments of individual children. Third, when teachers are shown to have differentiating practices, these have more frequently been related to unsubstantiated teacher expectations rather than children's educational needs (see Chapter 6 for a discussion of criteria for grouping children). The more recent emphasis on the value of whole class teaching has further eroded teachers' planning to meet individual needs. While both the national literacy and numeracy strategies emphasize the importance of differentiated questioning and some teachers are highly skilled at this, it remains the case that more whole class teaching has resulted in many children receiving the same undifferentiated diet. Whole class teaching is not as appropriate for younger children as it is for older ones. Sitting still and engaging in relatively passive, teacher-initiated learning takes a level of physical control and concentration that is simply too much for many 3- and 4-year-olds to manage. This is not to say that whole class experiences do not have a meaningful place in early education, but they must not take the place of experiences that specialist educators know would be more effective in smaller, more intimate circumstances.

As differentiation is so critical to children's development and progress, however, it is important that teachers clarify what elements of their planning can be matched more closely to children's differing needs. Differentiation may be concerned with:

- the *concepts, skills, knowledge and attitudes* that are the intended outcomes of an activity/experience;
- whether these concepts are to be introduced/developed/consolidated (the *spiral curriculum*);
- the *activity* itself – different activities can be vehicles for the same outcomes and differ according to the interests of the children;

- the *introduction* of an activity – more or less detailed, verbal or written etc.;
- the *process* of an activity, determined by the importance of the outcome, not necessarily uniform, but open to the most effective strategy for the child/group;
- the *outcome* of an activity, determined by the importance of the process; it may be open to interpretation by the child/group;
- the *support* given to an activity by an adult or other children, which may be minimal or substantial;
- the *resources* planned – different levels and different kinds;
- the *evidence* of learning, which varies according to the intended outcomes;
- the *collection* of evidence – which technique, by whom, when;
- the *assessment* of work – by the adult, child or both;
- by whose *criteria* the assessment takes place – adult, child or both;
- follow-up *action* – what, for whom, how, when.

There is no need for every element of this process to be addressed on every occasion, but it is important that all of these elements are open to change and adaptation in order to make learning experiences relevant, meaningful and effective for children. Sometimes the teacher plans for differentiation before an activity takes place – that is *differentiation by input*. Sometimes the activity is planned in such a way that it is appropriate for all children and the differentiation is seen in the way in which individuals respond to and learn from the activity – that is *differentiation by outcome*. A prompt sheet for supporting the planning of differentiated activities is given on pages 59–60. Rather than offering a format for short-term planning, I think a prompt sheet is more helpful so that, irrespective of the format that suits the individual teacher, plans can be checked against certain indicators of differentiation. Box 3.3 is offered as a starting point. You may find it helpful to formulate your own list with colleagues from your setting.

Conclusion

This chapter has been concerned with planning a curriculum that acknowledges the developmental needs of children within

Box 3.3   Short-term plans

Intended learning outcomes

- Why are the children doing this activity (from medium-term plans)?
- What do I intend that they should learn?
- What concepts/skills/knowledge/attitudes are to be introduced/developed/consolidated?

Play/activity/experience

- What play/activity/experiences will meet the intended learning outcomes?
- Do the children all need the same play/activity/experiences?
- Do I need to differentiate the introduction/the process/the outcome?
- Who will give the support or will children work independently?
- What grouping is most appropriate?
- What resources are needed? Are they the same for all children?
- Does the play/activity/experience meet the learning requirements of children with special needs?

Assessment

- What evidence do I need to gather?
- Will this enable me to assess the intended learning outcomes of the play/activity/experience?
- Is it possible to gain my evidence through first-hand observation or through conversations with children?
- Will this be done during or after the play/activity/experience?
- If evidence is to be recorded by an adult, what vocabulary, actions, behaviours are they looking for? How will the adult record this?
- If evidence is to be recorded by children will they be able to select their own method of recording and then explain it to an adult or their peers?
- Should samples of work be saved or photographs or tape recordings taken?

- What method of assessment will be most appropriate for the play/activity/experience planned?
- In what way might children be involved in assessing their own work?
- Were the intended learning outcomes achieved?
- If not, why not? What do I need to change?
- If the learning was not what I expected, what *did* I learn about the children from the outcomes of the activity?

NB be prepared to note unplanned and unexpected assessments too!

Action

- Do I need to change my short-term planning?
- Does a child/group/the class need to revisit a concept or have further practice of a skill?
- Should a child/the children have experience of working with a different child/children?
- Does a child/group need more support at the next stage of development?
- Does the child/group need different resources to support their learning?

the constraints of an externally imposed framework. It has been suggested that this is most easily done when long-term and medium-term planning are seen as meeting the development of the *curriculum* and short-term planning is seen as meeting the development of the *child*. An early years curriculum is concerned with process above product, as is demonstrated in the Stepping Stones in *The Curriculum Guidance for the Foundation Stage* (QCA/DfEE 2000) and fortunately, in most of the programmes of study at Key Stage 1. An appropriate curriculum is one that meets the needs and interests of children and also introduces children to a range of skills and concepts that are deemed, by adults, to be relevant and desirable for their education. The task of the teacher is to fuse together these dual interests and to ensure that the balance of children's experiences do not lead them to believe that education is something that is imposed by somebody else. Education should be a dynamic and liberating experience. If

children are to be life-long learners then the seeds for their independence and self-motivation to learn must be sown in their
earliest days of the school experience. The next chapter examines how teachers achieve a balance in classroom activities and
explores the role that teachers adopt in supporting the development of competent young learners.

4

THE ROLE OF THE TEACHER

Making the best use of teaching time

Introduction

The role of the teacher is inextricably bound up with how children are viewed as learners. As has already been shown, once it is acknowledged that children are competent (albeit inexperienced) learners, then teachers must be responsive to their varied and various abilities. Whatever it is intended that children should learn and however it is intended that they should learn it, the most effective learning is rooted in previous experience (Donaldson 1978; Wood 1988; Meadows 1993). Children are active learners, constantly constructing their own internal model of the world (Wells 1986; Wood 1988; Bronson 2000; Kuhn 2000). By acknowledging this, the teacher rejects a 'transmission' approach to teaching where the teacher is seen as having or having access to knowledge and skills which it is their responsibility to transmit to the learner. Instead, the teacher adopts what Rowland (1984: 4) describes as an 'interpretive' model of teaching, which involves 'not only the child's attempt to interpret and assimilate the knowledge and skills offered by the teacher, but also the teacher's growing understandings of the world'.

If we ignore what children already know and can do then their learning will not be embedded in what is already secure and what already makes sense to them. This sends messages to children that their competencies and contributions are not valued and this in turn can have a serious impact on their self-esteem.

The teacher as observer

We saw in Chapter 2 that in order to incorporate what children already know and can do teachers need to spend a considerable amount of time finding out what that is. Time for observation needs to be found not just at the beginning of the school year or term but throughout each teaching day so that planning is constantly informed by observations of children in action as learners. The problem for many teachers is that sitting still, not obviously engaged in interaction with a child or group of children, seems to be almost immoral! Teachers are so used to orchestrating a myriad of different activities all at the same time and being immersed in the action, that sitting back and simply watching children at work goes against the grain. Time for observation is critical, however. If teachers do not watch children at work then many important moments in their development and understanding may be missed. Of course teachers can and do make observations of children when they are working alongside them, but the nature of these observations is different. Children react and respond in different ways when teachers work alongside them, and if teachers want to see how children work independently or alongside their peers then they need to remove themselves from the situation and not be distracted by having more than one role at that particular time.

Making time for observation may seem daunting, but without time being set aside for focused observation of children at work teachers will not collect sufficient information about children as learners and planning will not be rooted in strong enough evidence of what children know and can do. Teachers who spend a significant amount of their time observing children say that the knowledge they gain enables them to plan far more appropriately for the individual child, group or class the next day or week. Time is not wasted in working with a child or group on an activity that is too easy or too difficult and time is not wasted in repeating or revisiting work unnecessarily. Time is actually *saved*, because the teacher is able to differentiate her planning on the basis of her increased knowledge about the children in her class.

Teachers need to make time to observe children during the teaching day. As with so many things in the classroom, it is a question of prioritizing time, but if time spent on observation saves time in planning and teaching and makes these more effective, then it is time well spent. One successful way that making time for observation can be achieved is by setting time aside at the short-term planning stage when decisions are being made about which activities the teacher is going to work with most closely – I call these *teacher-intensive* activities.

Teachers are all too aware of how short the school day is and the planning of their own time needs to be undertaken carefully. It also needs to be realistic. Teacher planning needs to create time for observation rather than it being fitted into snatched moments in the day. One way of achieving this is to identify on the teacher's daily plans first what/who is to be *taught* and second, what/who is to be *observed*. In this way, the teacher can see whether, given the time available, the two sets of teacher activities can be realistically achieved. As we have seen, observation is a critical part of the teaching process. The planning of the curriculum is informed by the observations that teachers make, and such an important process takes time. Planning for observation in this deliberate way may mean that time is taken from time that was previously set aside for direct involvement with children. Observation is part of the role of the teacher, however; it can only be done when children are at work or play and it should regularly be done when children are working independently of the teacher. Having a recorded plan that shows both the teaching and observation tasks for the day can help teachers to raise the status of classroom observation and give it the time it needs.

The teacher as 'teacher'

Making good use of time does not, of course, only apply to observation. A teacher has many roles to fulfil and very little time to spend. When looking to make the best use of teaching time it is necessary to be realistic. If a classroom situation is such that there is one teacher and possibly 20 or 30 children then the teacher has one of two choices. The easiest option is to teach the class as though it were a single unit, delivering the same curriculum to all children at the same time. This means that the class size is relatively immaterial because the onus is on the children to receive and inwardly digest the curriculum. Any teacher knows, however, that this will not guarantee *learning*. The same diet of experiences can be delivered to a class of children and their digestion of those experiences will be different. Some children will go hungry, some will end up feeling sick, some will turn up their noses because they don't like what's on offer and some will eat the bits they enjoy and leave the rest on the plate. It is the very fact that children cannot be neatly fitted into a curriculum but need a curriculum that fits *them* that makes teaching so challenging.

There are times when effective teaching and learning happens in a large group. The sharing of a big book, discussions about personal experiences and feelings, planning for a visitor or singing number rhymes all can be beneficial and effective as a whole-class experience. However, for the majority of their time in class, young children need to work – individually, in pairs or in groups – on activities that they will carry out independently. Such activities need to be sustained by individuals or groups so they do not need to interrupt the teacher at work with his or her teacher-intensive activity. These more independent activities I call teacher-initiated activities. In an early years classroom then, there are usually two main types of activity going on at any one time, which have been instigated by the teacher:

- *teacher-intensive activities:* these are activities in which the teacher is directly and constantly engaged with children;
- *teacher-initiated activities:* these are activities which the teacher initiates, but which the children will work on largely independently.

Teacher-intensive activities

Reports on classroom practice highlight the necessity for teachers to spend *focused* time with the child/children with whom they are working. For example, the HMI response (Ofsted 1993a) to the discussion paper by the 'Three Wise Men' (Alexander *et al.* 1992), identifies 'teaching targeted to specific individuals or groups' as one factor associated with better classroom practice. The national literacy and numeracy strategies rightly emphasize direct teaching as an essential part of the menu of children's learning opportunities. So, if focused time is being given to only some of the class then the important question is, what are the rest of the children doing? Planning for and working with the teacher-intensive group is not the problem. Planning for and ensuring the quality of the activities of the rest of the class is. Teachers have become increasingly skilled at planning the intended learning for a group, and teaching to that intended learning effectively. However, the effectiveness of planning for children to learn independently still needs considerable improvement in many classrooms.

Teacher-initiated activities

The first step towards addressing this issue comes from realizing that the nature of what children do when they are working with a teacher is significantly different from the nature of an activity when children work without the teacher. Activities that children will be doing independently are not simply the same as teacher-intensive activities but without the teacher there. Teacher-initiated activities differ from teacher-intensive activities in various ways.

Teacher-initiated activities need to:

- be sufficiently *clear* for children to be able to work without constantly checking that what they are doing is 'right';
- be sufficiently *motivating* that they will sustain the interest and involvement of the children so that they do not interrupt the teacher;
- involve an element of *problem-solving* so that children do not quickly come up with 'right answers';
- be sufficiently *open-ended* for children to be able to extend them in ways that interest and engage them.

The key is the open-endedness. The minute that an activity is so tightly prescribed by a teacher that there is clearly only one way of doing it – and that's the teacher's way – then children will repeatedly come to check that what they are doing is 'right'. If teachers want uninterrupted teaching time for teacher-intensive activities, then a great deal of consideration needs to be given to these activities which children are to undertake independently.

This does not mean of course that the teacher will not go to the children working on these teacher-initiated activities and have conversations with them about their work and answer their questions, but this will be done *when the teacher decides*. The teacher should be in control of his or her own time. This checking on activities – 'spinning the plates' as it is sometimes called – will occur after the teacher has finished one intensive activity and before starting the next. There is a world of difference between teachers being in control of when they move from one role to the next and being at the mercy of the children, doing little more than servicing their needs, because the planned activities all need teacher input at much the same level at much the same time.

Most of the children in an early years classroom will, most of the time, be working independently, so it is crucial that the activities in which they are engaged are worthwhile and bring about effective learning. Many children spend far too much of their school day on independent activities for these to be mere time-fillers. It is necessary to challenge the notion that the only worthwhile learning occurs when a teacher is there. This implies that any learning that occurs when children are working independently is of little value and this patently is not true, for we have already seen that the learning which children achieve prior to receiving any kind of formal education is very effective and usually self-driven. Children are learning all the time . . . and only a small amount of that time is spent anywhere near a teacher!

Child-initiated activity

There is a third kind of activity that should take place in every early years classroom and that is activity that is initiated by the child. Child-initiated activities encourage children to make their own choices and decisions about what they will do, the resources and equipment they will use and the processes and outcomes of the experience. This is *not* the kind of activity where a teacher encourages the children to use 'play equipment', such as plastic construction materials, and then gives them a specific task to complete with that material. This is a perfectly valid kind of activity, but it is not child-initiated. The minute a teacher has a planned intention for an activity, and directs either the process or the outcome, then that activity becomes teacher-initiated. Child-initiated activities enable children to be in control and to decide on experiences that are meaningful for them.

The place of child-initiated activity is central to the acknowledgement of children as competent learners. It is through such activity that young children make sense of their world, and learn to explore, experiment and take risks (Moyles 1989). The place of play is fully explored in Chapter 7, but suffice to say in this context that child-initiated activity should be part of the fabric of early years classrooms and is critical in the balance of activities that the teacher plans.

The balance of classroom activities

In the early years classroom then, there should be a balance between these three types of activity – teacher-intensive, teacher-initiated and child-initiated. I find it helpful to see these three types of activity as the three corners of a triangle (see Figure 4.1). The differences between the three activities can be summarized as follows:

- *child-initiated:* activity that children control in terms of experience, time and resources;
- *teacher-initiated:* activities that arise from adult planning; sufficiently open-ended for children to work on independently until the adult is ready to intervene;
- *teacher-intensive:* individual, pair or group work, usually differentiated by input; the focus of teacher time.

How the balance is maintained between these three types of activity will rest with the teacher and will change from day to day and sometimes session to session. It will certainly change according to the age of the children, because the younger the children the more the emphasis needs to be on child-initiated learning. What is powerful about this triangle model is that it works for whatever kind of learning situation is planned. It makes no difference whether children are engaged in an integrated day – experiencing different areas of learning simultaneously – or in a session where all the children are engaged in mathematical experiences at the same time. The principle of needing a balance of activities within an early learning environment still applies. Children need to experience the range of different learning

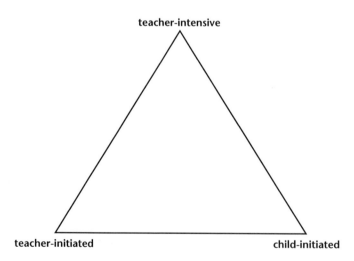

Figure 4.1   The balance of classroom activity

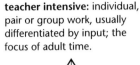

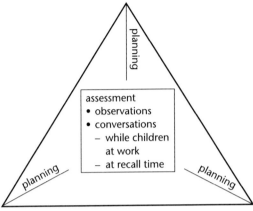

teacher intensive: individual, pair or group work, usually differentiated by input; the focus of adult time.

planning

assessment
• observations
• conversations
  – while children at work
  – at recall time

planning

planning

independent, not abandoned, learning

teacher initiated: activities that arise from teacher planning; sufficiently open-ended for children to work on independently until the teacher is ready to intervene.

child initiated: activities that children control in terms of experience, time and resources.

Figure 4.2   The balance of learning and teaching in the foundation stage class

opportunities offered by teacher-intensive, teacher-initiated and child-initiated learning and adults need to make best use of their time by planning activities that make different demands on the level of their involvement with different groups. Looking at classroom activities in this way helps to see what can reasonably be managed and addresses, in a positive and professional way, what the rest of the class is doing. The movement of the teacher between these activities can be summarized as follows:

1 The teacher works with an individual or small group on a teacher-intensive task.
2 The rest of the class is engaged on either teacher-initiated or child-initiated activities.
3 These activities must enable children to be independent of the teacher so that they do not need to interrupt the teacher-intensive task.

4 The teacher completes the teacher-intensive task and moves to both the teacher-initiated and child-initiated activities in order to support and extend these experiences as appropriate.
5 Independent learning should not be abandoned learning. Teacher involvement in all classroom activities is crucial if they are to have status and purpose.
6 Once children working independently have been adequately supported, the teacher returns to the next teacher-intensive activity.
7 The rest of the class moves independently between teacher-initiated and child-initiated activities until/unless the teacher draws them to a teacher-intensive task. (How children move from one activity to the next is the subject of Chapter 9.)
8 *All* classroom activities are shared at a review time during the day (see Chapter 9).

Figure 4.2 summarizes these points and demonstrates the vital interaction between assessment, planning and teaching.

Use of teacher time

Looking at the balance between teacher-intensive, teacher-initiated and child-initiated learning gives each teacher action a clear purpose. Each role is planned, it is deliberate and, most of all, it acknowledges that a classroom with one teacher and 30 children has to be planned for realistically. I am not suggesting that, by using this management strategy, children will *never* interrupt! Some children – for justifiable reasons – will occasionally need help or reassurance, but by planning particularly teacher-initiated activities with care, the number of interruptions will be minimized. A culture of independence surfaces in the classroom, where children know that they do not need to rely on the teacher at every turn and they come to enjoy their autonomy.

The recorded interactions between a teacher and her reception class (Fisher 1996) provide fascinating data that chronicles the growing independence of children and the changes in their attitudes and behaviour towards their teacher. At the beginning of the school year, in the autumn term, the children related to the teacher in ways that revealed their dependence on her:

Do you want me to do any more?

Can I stop this now please?

As the children became more independent they seem to revise their concept of what 'being a pupil' meant, started to revel in their new-found independence and ignored the teacher almost completely. During the spring term the teacher was often left alone for 15–25 minutes without interruption, allowing her to get on with her teacher-intensive activities. Then, towards the end of the spring term the relationship changed once again and the children began to refer back to the teacher, but the nature of the exchanges had altered. The children were no longer seeking reassurance, but were coming to their teacher simply to share the pleasure of a discovery or an achievement or specifically to request her support:

Do you want to see the model I've made?

Child: I can't do my 'a's.
Teacher: Do you want me to help?
Child: Yes.

Can you help me finish the story I'm writing?

The children's perceptions of the role of the teacher had changed. Because they had independence and a considerable degree of autonomy in the classroom, it seemed as though they came to see the teacher as yet another valuable resource to enable them to complete their tasks in hand.

Differentiation

Child-initiated activities will be, by their very nature, differentiated by outcome. Children's own decisions about activities are a reflection of their ability, their knowledge, their understanding and their skill. Observation of these activities will inform the teacher of them, and of the child's attitudes and motivation. They show the child's confidence and self-esteem, their perseverance and persistence and their willingness to try new things or their need to repeat what is familiar.

Teacher-initiated activities are best planned so that differentiation will be by outcome. Sometimes it is appropriate that an activity is planned for a group of children of certain ability and that this activity is exclusively for them. More often than not, however, the very nature of an open-ended, problem-solving task is that children will tackle the task at their own level. As long as there is no 'right answer' and children know that their own solution will be valued, then the same task for a range of children is – in this instance – preferable. Differentiation by outcome places an emphasis on the teacher learning *about* children through the selected activity, as much as children learning *from* the activity.

Teacher-intensive activities are most likely to be differentiated by input. In other words, the teacher has planned to work with a group of children who have reached the same stage at the same time and will benefit from being introduced to, or consolidating, or revisiting an activity, task or experience together. The teacher's knowledge of the needs of these children will have come directly from his or her first-hand observations of them at work independently and as they work with adults.

Independent learning

Several groups of students and school staffs with whom I have worked have found it very beneficial to explore the nature of teacher-initiated activities. Working together and sharing subject expertise, groups of practitioners can brainstorm experiences/activities across all curriculum areas, which they believe to be worthwhile independent learning opportunities for children. These experiences/activities are then shared and the group debates whether and at what point children will have recourse to an adult. Some staffs have then compiled their own bank of such activities, amending and commenting on those that work particularly well or those that did not produce the independence anticipated.

Worksheets

We cannot leave the subject of independent learning without addressing, head on, the issue of worksheets. Sometimes teachers feel they need written evidence that something has been learnt, and I hope that Chapter 2 has dispelled that particular myth. For more than any other reason, worksheets are given to children to keep them occupied while the teacher does other things. My emphasis on the importance of teacher-initiated activities should demonstrate that independent learning must be both dynamic and purposeful. I would suggest that worksheets are neither of these things. When tempted to offer a worksheet to a young child, the following issues should be contemplated:

1 The difference between many children's literacy skills and their conceptual understanding is great. It is possible for children to have a relatively sophisticated understanding of a concept and yet be unable to record this because the worksheet uses language that they cannot read or don't understand or their own written language is not sufficiently developed.

2 Worksheet answers can be copied or guessed at. Since so many of them require gaps to be filled in, the chances of doing either or both are quite high. All this may give evidence of, is how able another child is on the same table.

3 A worksheet restricts what a young child can tell you about what they know and understand. If children devise their own ways of recording knowledge and understanding then they will select ways that make sense to them and that give all the information they want to share.

4 Worksheets clone children into producing the same answers to fill in uniform gaps.

5 Children frequently spend more time colouring in worksheets than they do engaging with the concepts behind them. By the time the worksheet is finished most young children are hard pushed to tell you what it was about.

6 Young children spend far *less* time completing most worksheets than teachers spend laboriously drawing – or photocopying – them.

It is unreasonable to criticize things without offering viable alternatives, so:

- if *evidence of learning* is needed, *watch* and *listen* to the child and record what they do and say;
- if *recorded evidence* is needed, let the child devise their own ways of recording;
- if *time-fillers* are needed, think again; address the issue of independent learning positively and initiate activities that are valuable and valid.

Motivation and perseverance

One of the greatest benefits to the teacher of encouraging independent learners is that, by and large, children remain motivated learners. This means that a teacher spends less time coercing children to complete a directed task, something that takes up both time and energy. It also means that children usually remain on task for longer and therefore are less likely to make demands on teacher time, which is an added bonus. Children, like adults, lack concentration when they are required to do something that they find meaningless and irrelevant. All too often this can happen when the activities that teachers plan do not take account of children's own experiences and interests. Not that children should only ever engage in activities they *choose* to, but how much easier it is – for both children and adults – when children are motivated to pursue a task rather than having to be coerced to do so. Successful teachers 'go with the flow' of children, capturing and using their current interests and absorptions to plan the curriculum. If children's experiences are not embedded in their current needs and interests then an activity can appear pointless to them and they either rush to finish it or simply do not give it adequate attention. This is when teachers get interrupted with cries of 'I've finished!'. . . and all teachers know how aggravating *that* can be.

Status and quality

Some teachers are concerned that giving children too much independence will result in work of inferior quality. There are a number of ways of ensuring that this is not the case and most of these hinge on the teacher's own attitudes to the activities that are going on in the classroom. In order for children to value their own work, whether it is teacher-intensive, teacher-initiated or child-initiated, it has to have status. Status can be conferred by the child and their own involvement and pride in their efforts and ideas. Status is also conferred by the teacher, however, who confirms or denies the importance of different activities through a myriad of different messages – given both explicitly and implicitly. All classroom activities should be worthwhile. If they are not, then they should be given houseroom. Teacher-intensive, teacher-initiated and child-initiated activities should all be of value to the teacher and to the children, and should all be planned for specific learning purposes. The three kinds of activity will be given equal status if they are:

- *happening at the same time* as each other, not one always preceding the others because it is seen by the teacher as being more important;

- *observed, monitored and assessed* by the teacher when children are in action;
- *the subject of conversations* in order to find out what children have done and discovered, and to show interest in their efforts and achievements where observation has not been possible;
- *used to inform future planning.*

In this way, the activities in the classroom all have a clear purpose and the use of precious teaching time is maximized.

Conclusion

The role the teacher adopts in the classroom is the key to the quality of experiences planned for the child in school. If teachers are to emulate the success of children's early educators, then their role will be most successful when they facilitate and support children's learning and respond to what children initiate (Sharp 2000). Formal education has a further dimension, however. Teachers are responsible for transmitting the values of society and introducing children to areas of learning and experience that they might not otherwise discover for themselves. Even so, learning is most successful when the strategies that teachers use enable children to own the experiences as much as possible and to see the relevance of those experiences to their own lives.

Teachers manage a complex orchestration of activities within the classroom. What is critical to remember is that when involved in early years education, teachers will not be directly teaching all of the children all of the time. Indeed the reality of the situation is that more children will spend more of their school day working independently than they will working with a teacher. It is vital then for teachers to focus their attention on those activities that encourage independence and autonomy. They should be demanding and challenging and not planned in order to fill in time until the teacher is free. By looking at the balance between teacher-intensive, teacher-initiated and child-initiated activities, teachers can make their role both responsive to the children's needs for independence and realistic in terms of their own need to spend targeted time with individuals and groups. The next chapter explores a variety of ways of encouraging children to be independent learners and considers how the classroom can be organized to facilitate this.

5

ENCOURAGING INDEPENDENCE

The effective use of space and resources

Introduction

Teachers who spend focused time scaffolding the learning of children and making regular observations of children in action have already created a classroom environment that encourages independence. Neither of these crucial teacher activities can be achieved satisfactorily if a teacher is constantly being interrupted with the well-worn cry 'Please miss...what do I do next?' In order for children to be independent learners they need a classroom environment that facilitates their independence. As far as possible, children need to manage their own resources, space and time. If children are to work independently, they need to be given systems and strategies that enable them to manage their own learning environment and sustain their own learning.

Children's early experiences

I have already suggested that to adopt effective strategies at school, we should examine more closely the learning environments in which children have spent time prior to starting school. In these environments, children have been successful learners because:

- the world around them is an interesting place;
- young children are naturally curious;
- children want to explore, to experiment and to become competent;

- in the home and the community there are countless opportunities to do this as and when children are inspired to do so;
- young children meet new and varied learning experiences in many contexts – the kitchen, the street, on the television, in the park;
- there is almost always an adult on hand to ask questions of and to learn from – responding to the child's queries and questioning.

The classroom learning environment needs, therefore, to provide the following elements:

- new and interesting experiences;
- activities that encourage children's natural curiosity;
- opportunities to explore, experiment and become competent;
- a timetable that is sufficiently flexible to give the children some control over when and how experiences/activities/tasks are carried out;
- learning that occurs in a range of contexts – the classroom, outside of the classroom, on visits, on trips, in workplaces, in the street;
- access to adults and other expert and experienced people (including other children) who will answer and raise questions and pose challenges to extend learning and understanding.

Creating an environment for independent learners

To begin with, the classroom environment must be appropriately designed in terms of *space* and *resources.*

Space

When teachers think about what they would like to have in their classrooms to stimulate and extend children's learning, they usually find there simply is not enough space. In discussion with a group of experienced reception and Key Stage 1 teachers about what they would *ideally* like to have in their classrooms, the following list emerged:

The indoor area

- carpeted area(s) for:
  - sharing work,
  - jigsaws,

- games,
- construction,
- grouping together;
- home/imaginative/role play area;
- sand tray(s) – wet and/or dry;
- water tray;
- interest/discovery/exploratory area;
- bed for children to rest;
- quiet area;
- writing/mark-making area;
- reading area;
- listening area;
- music area;
- table tops;
- creative area:
  - gluing,
  - painting,
  - cutting,
  - dough,
  - clay,
  - plasticine,
  - modelling;
- computer area.

The outdoor area

- a garden area;
- trees, bushes and seats;
- large apparatus;
- an area for small apparatus, for example hoops, bean bags;
- an area for bikes, tricycles and trucks;
- a *large* sand pit;
- an area for water play;
- an area for construction;
- an area for imaginative play;
- an area, in shade, for mark-making, reading and talking.

It might be useful to draw up your own list about what you believe young children would benefit from in their learning environment at school. I suspect the lists would be very similar –

and equally long. In doing this exercise it is important to concentrate on what children *need* and not, as yet, on the constraints of making this a reality. The chances are that there will not be enough space in any one classroom for all of these areas and experiences. So how should decisions be made about what to leave in and what to take out?

The most important question for teachers to ask is, what do young learners need most? This should provide the foundation for all other decisions that will be made. Sometimes it is all too easy to be distracted by other issues. All the other classrooms in the school have this or that in them; the school has always been organized like x or y; the caretaker hates clearing up sand . . . and so on. At the end of the day, however, teachers are concerned with what is in the best interests of children and should not be swayed from using this as their yardstick. Almost inevitably, some areas will have to be left out . . . or at best rotated with other less important areas. However those areas that the teacher has deemed to be invaluable will form the basis of the learning experiences of children and the decisions will have been made using the teacher's professional knowledge about the learning needs of young children.

In many early years classrooms, the majority of space is taken up by tables and chairs. Before decisions are made about prioritizing the use of the rest of the space, it is important to consider whether space given to a table and chair for every child is space well used. Bearing in mind the need for young children to engage in active learning and practical, first-hand experiences, it is worth giving some thought to the following issues:

- tables and chairs take up a great deal of floor space;
- the removal of *one* set of tables and six to eight chairs could create space for:
  - a sand or water tray,
  - a carpet area,
  - an investigation/interactive area,
  - a listening area etc.;
- any one of these areas might be in use for *most* of the school day;
- are tables and chairs, for every child at the same time, needed for *most* of the school day or only occasionally?
- which use of space is most valuable for the young learner?

Box 5.1   Making decisions about the use of space

- draw up a list of those areas that are valuable for young learners;
- prioritize them in order to make adjustments for the available space;
- eliminate those that are of little value or seldom used;
- plan the remaining areas within the space available;
- be able to justify decisions on sound educational grounds.

The same range of questions can be asked about almost all compromise situations in the use of classroom space:

- Why is this taking up space?
- Could the space be better used?
- Could this be removed?
- Who shall I get to help me?

What is eliminated should be judged less important than what remains. Teachers may need to justify their decisions to a range of people, but those decisions will be taken on more solid ground if the justification for them is that they are in the best interests of young learners.

Allocating space

Once a list of areas is established it is helpful to plan these so that the learning environment encourages purposeful, interactive experiences. It is a good idea to experiment with possible design layouts on paper *before* starting to move heavy pieces of furniture around the room!

Once the areas are allocated space, then these can be named and, if appropriate, labelled, so that the children are clear about what areas are appropriate for what activity. The naming and labelling gives a sense of order to what can otherwise be a very confusing environment. It might help to imagine going into an unfamiliar supermarket and looking for the washing powders or the cereals without signs identifying where these are to be found. Clearly identified classroom areas make the organization and the management of the learning environment so much more straightforward for both teachers, helpers and children.

Box 5.2   Principles about using space

- some areas will be determined by fixtures such as sinks and floor surfaces and these need allocating first;
- each area needs sufficient space for children to move around comfortably and safely;
- some learning experiences naturally benefit from being placed alongside others, for example the home corner can extend to a café which can benefit from being near the block play area for interrelated play;
- some areas benefit from *not* being near others, for example the listening area or book corner will probably be disturbed by the activity in the construction area;
- there need to be areas where children can work independently, in small groups and as a large group.

Resources

Once space has been allocated then all the resources that will be needed in any one area should be made available. Children who are going to be independent in their learning need to know where to find resources and where to return them once they have been used.

The choice of activities should once again be determined by the needs of the young learner. If we want children to continue to explore, investigate and discover then we should select resources and equipment that enable this to go on. Sometimes the resources that offer some of the greatest learning potential are the most expensive. Wooden blocks, for example, may seem expensive to those operating on a slim budget, but if they provide children with a wealth of experiences in aesthetics, mathematics, the processes of science and problem-solving (Gura 1992), then they offer good value for money.

Money can be wasted on resources that might preferably be replaced by *natural* resources that take time rather than money to collect. A Sunday afternoon walk, a visit to relatives or an outing to certain shops can result in a whole host of wonderful resources for sorting, printing, selling, describing or investigating.

The first task in most classrooms is to *gather together* what already exists – and then be quite ruthless with anything that is out of date, inappropriate or has pieces missing. Space is at a premium in classrooms and everything that is in it should be relevant, necessary and in one piece!

It can sometimes be very difficult for teachers to get rid of things, especially if they have been accumulating them 'just in case'. If there is unlimited space and these resources are not making the place look too untidy then, of course, they can be kept. But if keeping some things means there is no space for others, or it is difficult to find or reach others, then the needs of the learners in your classroom should be prioritized. *Throw out* the least useful resources, and those kept 'just in case'. One rule of thumb can be that if something has not been used in the course of a full academic year it will either be thrown away or given to someone for whom it *is* appropriate and who *will* use it.

Once all unnecessary clutter has been disposed of, it is possible to *identify the gaps* in the available resources and decisions can be made about what needs to be added or ordered. There are many resources that can be found or scrounged rather than bought, but however resources are gathered, there are certain principles to bear in mind (see Box 5.3).

Having selected and gathered new resources together, these need to be sorted and *allocated* to the areas in the classroom in

---

Box 5.3   Principles about gathering resources

- resources should be appropriate for both the girls and the boys in your class;
- resources should encourage girls to play in areas that are traditionally the domain of boys and vice versa, for example clothes in the dressing up area that will attract boys to role-play;
- resources should reflect a wide range of cultures whether they are represented by the ethnic mix in the class or not; these might include jigsaws, cooking utensils in the home corner or books;
- resources should be appropriate for a range of special needs, interests and circumstances no child should feel excluded from an activity or experience because the resources available reflect a cultural, gender, social or ability bias.

which they are most appropriate. It is particularly important that the children see the significance of this sorting process. As with many other stages of this organization of space and resources, the children can be valuably involved in the process and this will be explored later. At this point, it is sufficient to suggest that adults should not make assumptions about what is 'logical' to children. There are a number of resources that can be of use in more than one curriculum area. Therefore will the allocation be made on the basis of most frequent use or most logical use? Will there be a resource area for each area of learning or is this unrealistic? Is it best to divide curriculum resources between three major areas as suggested by Janet Moyles (1992)?

- *investigation area*: essentially science, maths, technology;
- *language area*: mainly English, history, geography;
- *creative area*: mostly art, design, music.

There are no hard and fast rules about organization. What *is* important, is that the decisions that are made make sense to the children who will use them, as well as the adults, and that the classroom systems are consistently applied. In this way, resources are more likely to be found and replaced without confusion.

Once the resources have been allocated to a certain area they can be *labelled* for further ease of finding and returning. Some teachers label both the *resource* and the *location* so that even the youngest children can match the item to its correct home. The labelling can be appropriate to the age and ability of the children using them. The label may be a picture that a child or adult has drawn; it may be a catalogue picture that has been cut out; it may be a word describing the resource; it may be a coloured symbol denoting a certain category of resource. Alternatively, a headteacher colleague I know and respect feels that it is better that children come to learn where things go *without* such prompts. As with all things, this is a decision for individual teachers and their children. It is also a decision, along with others to do with classroom management, that a whole staff might want to discuss. As with most aspects of an effective school, the shared discussion and decision-making within a staffroom can have a very positive impact on children's school experiences. If children are to be encouraged to be independent, then it is highly beneficial to them – and to their teachers – that there is a consistent approach throughout the school. Nothing could be more frustrating than being given independence and autonomy in one situation only to have it taken away in the next. So do raise these issues collaboratively with colleagues. If nursery children can manage the levels of independence visible in any good quality environment, then just imagine what 7-year-olds can achieve.

In order to facilitate independence, resources need to be located in *accessible* places. This has implications for the amount of resources in a classroom and is the reason for suggesting that cluttered resource areas are not helpful. If resources are cluttered, muddled, piled too high or too deep, then a child or adult may not be able to see a resource, let alone realize that it might be useful. They may know the resource is there somewhere, but be unable to find it and consequently might use something less helpful. Equally, they may not find a space to return it to or may feel that the space is in such a mess they can put it anywhere . . . and the space remains cluttered.

Resources are best placed on uncluttered surfaces that make them easy to be seen and easy to reach. This means that it is better not to have resources in cupboards with doors. Doors can hide a multitude of clutter and they also take up a lot of space. Cupboard doors have to have space in order to be opened and that space could be so much more effectively used if the doors were removed.

Finally, children and adults need to be *trained* to find and replace resources properly. I do not usually use the word 'train', but in this context I think it is appropriate. By train I mean, 'reminded repeatedly so that it becomes habit'. It will not happen by chance, neither will it happen instantly! Children need regular reminding about where resources are to be found, how to use them and where to put them back. This is particularly true if you are a reception class teacher with fresh intakes of children throughout the school year. Such strategies are best made into part of the daily classroom routine, particularly for younger children, so that at some point in each day they watch while someone finds/replaces a certain piece of equipment or resource. This can serve two useful purposes. First, it reinforces the importance of 'a place for everything and everything in its place' and how necessary that is for a space that is being used by a lot of people. Second, it is valuable to remind children of what resources *are* available, so that they can include them in their activities as appropriate. Young children need to develop an awareness of their role in the care of the environment, not just within school but outside in the community also. They will learn the basic

> **Box 5.4   Planning and arranging resources**
>
> - *collect* all existing resources together;
> - *throw out* all those that are incomplete and/or inappropriate;
> - *gather together* new/necessary resources;
> - *sort* into categories that fit the arrangement of the room;
> - *label* by object, catalogue picture, word (possibly label re-source *and* location);
> - *locate* resources on accessible, open shelving;
> - *train* children to locate and return all resources themselves.

tenets of respect and value for the world around them if there is an ethos in the classroom that expects and encourages them to care for and be responsible for their own learning environment.

Finally, children need to be given *time* at the end of sessions to be responsible for *sorting and tidying* their own areas and activities so that they learn to be responsible for their own learning environment and appreciate the necessity, for everyone's sake, to keep it an organized and efficient working environment. One very helpful strategy is to give children a five-minute warning. If children are told that they have five minutes before they will be asked to stop what they are doing then it not only gives them the opportunity to start clearing away, but it also gives them time to finish off or to stop an activity at a point that is more appropriate to *them* rather than instantly because the teacher has (for example) found 'we're already late for assembly'.

The outdoor area

The outdoor area is a critical part of the learning environment for children. If we return to the suggestion that the school environment should mirror the successful learning environment of the preschool child's experiences then discovering and exploring out of doors clearly offers children new and exciting experiences to stimulate their interest and arouse their curiosity. All too often in school settings, the outdoor learning environment has been reduced to a playground, and what this actually means in practice is that children are sent out of doors simply to let off steam. Even designated outdoor learning areas are sometimes seen this way, and not viewed 'as a combined learning environment worthy of as much thought, effort and capital as the indoor learning environment' (Bilton 1994: 35).

A good early years curriculum acknowledges the value of a learning environment both indoors and outdoors, and should provide for the flow of learning between the two environments. The highly informative ILEA document *A Curriculum for Young Children: Outdoor Play* (1990: 6) identifies three different ways of linking the indoor and outdoor environments:

1 the inside can be *transferred* outside – that is elements from the inside are physically moved outside – like rebuilding the home corner outdoors;
2 the provision is *linked* or *paralleled* – for instance, inside water play using tubes and bottles to move water can be paralleled outside using guttering, drainpipes and buckets;
3 an outside activity can be *contrasted* with an activity indoors – small-scale painting inside can be contrasted with the use of large sheets of paper and decorating brushes outside.

Designing an outdoor area

Clearly the design of an outdoor learning environment will be dependent on whether or not the classroom has direct access to the outdoors and what opportunities lie outside. Having said that, most classrooms could make better use of the available space – such as it is – than they currently do. It is important to explore the possibilities and to take on board whatever is feasible while lobbying for greater provision.

An outdoor learning environment should have:

- a landscape with:
  - grassed areas and hard surface areas,
  - tracks using different surfaces, e.g. bricks, cobblestones,
  - shaded areas and sunlit areas,
  - places to run and places to sit,
  - areas to cultivate and areas in which to encourage natural habitats,
  - trees, shrubs, bushes, flowers and vegetables,
  - animals and birds to care for;
- areas to encourage the development of gross motor skills:
  - swings and ropes,
  - slides,

- climbing frames,
- mats to jump on or over,
- structures for balancing and jumping between – all sited on appropriate safe surfaces,
- bicycles and tricycles,
- wagons and wheelbarrows to push and pull,
- scooters,
- bouncing and rocking equipment – and pathways to travel on without interrupting the activities of other children;

- activities that encourage fine motor development:
  - balls and bean bags,
  - hoops,
  - quoits,
  - wood area,
  - creative area,
  - small sand and water play area;

- resources that encourage exploration and discovery:
  - construction materials,
  - sand pit/tray(s),
  - water tray(s),
  - role-play props,
  - roadways and playmats,
  - design and creative materials,
  - unstructured materials,
  - music and rhythm materials;
  some teachers acquire large carpets that can be put on concrete outside the classroom to enable children to sit and work

- resources that encourage imagination and expression:
  - drapes for hideaways,
  - a garden shed,
  - boxes and crates,
  - masks, cloaks, hats and shoes,
  - puppets,
  - an old boat,
  - large wheels and long ropes.

Further points to consider include:

- *storage*: equipment and resources need to be stored so that children can be involved in getting things out and putting them away for themselves;

- *safety*: the play area must be fenced off and any entrances should be fitted with safety hooks;
- *the weather*: UK weather is not as bad as we sometimes imagine (just think how relatively few playtimes are lost to bad weather). The provision of a covered veranda – preferably wide enough to allow the use of wheeled toys – should protect the children from both extremes of temperature. The Danish early childhood educators say there is no such thing as bad weather – only bad clothing. Good quality provision offers children macs and boots to change into when going outside. Bad weather offers a wealth of learning opportunities that simply cannot be experienced if the weather is always fine. Just think what can be learnt through playing in puddles!
- *the role of the adult*: adults should work with children outdoors in just the same ways as they do indoors. They are there to facilitate, question, respond and extend children's learning. It is not a time merely for the 'supervision' of behaviour.

Eliminating the little things

In the course of a day there are many little things for which children interrupt teachers and waste their valuable professional time. It is useful to write down all the things that cause children to interrupt and that can become agitating, things like 'my pencil's blunt'; 'can I go to the toilet?'; 'we've run out of green paint'; 'I need some more glue'. Having written these down, it becomes easier to devise ways of eliminating the interruptions and to put classroom time aside to address the issues. This can be a fascinating theme for a staff meeting, when solutions can be jointly constructed.

If children learn to manage the little things in the learning environment then it can save them – and their teachers – valuable time. The important thing is to identify what these 'little things' are and then to set about systematically teaching the children to address them themselves. Given time and practice the youngest children are perfectly capable of mixing paints or sharpening pencils. Creating time for children to learn these skills can require a change of attitude for some teachers. It means providing the resources to enable children to manipulate them easily – appropriately sized and shaped pencil sharpeners for example. It also means allowing children the time and opportunity to find out for themselves that too much water means their pictures look wishy-washy. To become independent, children need to be taught certain skills and then given time to practise them. It is up to the teacher to set time aside in order to show children how to tie each others' aprons, cut paper, or find a new book. Showing children once is, of course, never enough. Experiences like these need repetition, building into the day – perhaps at whole class time or sharing time – so that children are constantly reminded of the classroom expectations and how to go about looking after themselves. As with many other classroom issues, time invested here will save time later on. In this instance, the time it will save is teacher time that can then be spent on the valuable business of *teaching* rather than *servicing*. Children feel a great sense of pride and personal achievement when they manage themselves and do not feel they have to go to an adult. The important thing is that children are taught the skills and strategies for independence and are then given opportunities to practise and use them. It is important too that the children's efforts are seen as valuable parts of the learning process.

Accidents do happen, however. Should the paint go on the floor or the water tray splash over, then valuable adult time can be wasted if it is the classroom expectation that it is an *adult* who clears it up. This, too, is something that – given appropriate training – children are perfectly capable of doing for themselves. The teacher simply needs to ensure that children have the wherewithal to clear up. It is helpful if, close to those areas that are prone to getting messy, there is a range of equipment for clearing up. Near the water tray, for example, there should be a mop and bucket and sponges; near the sand tray, a broom and dustpan and brush; near the painting table, more sponges, cloths and a supply of paper towels. It helps enormously if, where appropriate, these are child-sized. It helps the child to manipulate the equipment so much more easily and it gives a clear message that this is the province of the child and not something that an adult automatically manages on their behalf.

Involving children in making decisions

I suggested earlier that it can be beneficial for children to be involved in decisions about space and resources as much as is possible. We all know that, given a sense of ownership and a feeling of responsibility about something, then we are likely to take more interest and effort in maintaining it. There are other important reasons why involving children can be of value to them and their teachers. Involving children:

- gives opportunities for real-life problem solving;
- encourages children to maintain something that they have planned;
- enables children to have an element of control over their own learning environment;
- leads to the development of organization as a life skill;
- gives children a sense of responsibility/self esteem;
- encourages cooperation and collaboration between children and with adults;
- enables the teacher to see things from the children's perspectives.

Children can be involved in planning and arranging:

- the use of space;
- the naming of work areas;
- the selection of resources;
- the categorizing of resources;
- the sorting of resources;
- the labelling of resources;
- the location of resources.

Reviewing the use of space and resources

The design and management of a learning environment is an ongoing exercise. It requires both children and adults to review the classroom constantly as a learning environment and to be given opportunities for suggesting ways in which improvements can be made. The following are useful questions that teachers can ask children – and themselves:

Space
- Do children have room to move about the classroom without interfering in other children's activities?
- Is there space for children to engage in active learning?
- Is there space for a child to sit alone or with a friend as well as in a small group or in a large group?
- Is there space for a child to be quiet as well as to be interactive?

Resources
- Can children access resources without interfering with the activities of other children?
- Are resources clearly visible?
- Do resources get put back in the right place?
- Are there enough resources for everyone's needs?

Management
- How often are adults interrupted with queries that are not to do with teaching and learning?
- What is the nature of those interruptions?
- Do children know what to do if paint/paper/glue runs out?
- Do children know how to sharpen pencils?
- Do children know what to do if they need aprons/shoes tied?
- Do children know what to do if things are spilt?
- Do children know what to do with finished work?
- Do children know what to do when they have finished an activity?

Establishing independence

Encouraging children to be independent can take time, but it is time wisely spent. It is very hard to plan a teaching day where adults can spend quality time with individuals or groups of children if the rest of the class is not able to operate independently. It may well be that, rather than begin teaching the curriculum from day one, that teachers could spend the early days of a term or year teaching independence. Time can be put aside so that children are taught to find and replace resources, to mix paint, to sharpen pencils, to move from one activity to the next without recourse to an adult (see Chapter 9 for further details of this). The role of the adult during this time is to watch and help this growing independence. Teachers need to have the time to show a child how to do something or to remind them where to find something. This is best achieved if the teacher has not planned to spend this time teaching the curriculum. Any attempt to teach individuals or groups while children do not have independence is likely to lead to frustration. It may seem that the curriculum is so full that spending the first days of term not teaching it is not a sensible suggestion! However, establishing whole class independence – and seeing this as valuable teaching and learning in its own right – will be of long-term benefit to subsequent teaching and learning of the curriculum.

Teaching and learning independence is probably best achieved if children are engaged chiefly in *child-initiated* activities, that is, activities that children can sustain without recourse to an adult. This leaves the teacher free to concentrate on supporting independence rather than anything else. Once children are independent, *teacher-initiated* activities can be gradually introduced so that the teacher can see if children can sustain their independence while being required to work at certain prescribed tasks in the course of the day. The teacher still needs to leave sufficient breathing space for herself or himself to remind and support children when they come for help unnecessarily. When independence is established as a part of classroom life, then the full range of teacher-intensive, teacher-initiated and child-initiated activities can be introduced. This does not mean that children will never again interrupt the teacher, but it does mean that the times when this happens should be dramatically reduced, that children can feel responsible for their own learning and that the teacher is able to get on with the business of teaching.

Conclusion

Independent learners are a necessary part of classroom life. One teacher has too many children to be able to teach all of them directly, all of the time, and it is inevitable that children spend a large part of their classroom experience working alone. As we shall see in the next chapter, this is not only necessary but also desirable. Children working together, without adult supervision, is an important part of the curriculum, for when children work alongside their peers they develop many different skills and understandings. Learning to collaborate and cooperate is a life-long process and it is crucial that children have the opportunity to rehearse these skills when they are young. Chapter 6 is concerned with the importance of children working and learning with others; it examines the place of talk in the early years curriculum and challenges some established notions about group work.

6

COLLABORATION AND COOPERATION

The importance of talking and working with others

Introduction

One of the most important elements of an environment appropriate for young learners is the provision of opportunities for children to talk together, and with adults, as they work. There is now a powerful consensus about the centrality of talk to learning, a consensus brought about by the powerful findings of studies of language in the home and at school (significantly the Bristol study 'Language at home and at school' directed by Gordon Wells (1981, 1986), the research studies of Barbara Tizard and Martin Hughes (1984) and the work of the National Oracy Project). Studies such as these confirm that talking things through is an essential method by which we all make sense of our experience. Vygotsky (1962) saw how young children solve practical tasks with the help of their speech as well as their eyes and hands and use language as a way of sorting out their thoughts. At first, language and action are fused together in this way, and that is why young children are often heard talking to themselves when they are engaged in an activity. Eventually, language and action become separated and the activity can be represented in the medium of words (Bruner 1985).

The realization of the impact of language on thought and learning has had two significant influences on classroom practice. The first concerns talk between the children and the teacher:

to be most helpful, the child's experience of conversation should be in a one-to-one situation in which the adult is talking about matters that are of interest and concern to the child . . . or about activities in which the child and adult engage together.

(Wells 1985: 44)

The second influence concerns children and their peers and a response to the assertion that:

collaborative talk not only facilitates the task, it also empowers the learner. Indeed . . . it has the potential for promoting learning that exceeds that of almost any other type of talk.

(Chang and Wells 1988: 97)

Communication with adults

In the preschool years, talking and learning go hand in hand. Children communicate with adults and their siblings and peers about things that are of interest and concern to them. The strategies that children have developed for actively making sense of their experiences have, as we have seen, been highly effective. Yet once children go to school this model of active learning through talk is not always emulated. Instead, children very often meet the vestiges of the learning-by-listening model of teaching with few opportunities to engage in the kinds of dynamic interaction that might bring about the quality of learning described above. Tizard and Hughes (1984: 14) point out that comparisons between conversations at home and in the nursery reveal how differently children can behave in two settings, and that in some cases 'it is hard to believe it is the same child who is talking'. Teachers talk to children in two predominant contexts, first as individuals or as members of a small group, second in a larger context, as members of the whole class.

Talking to individuals

Conversations with individual children are a critical part of the teacher's repertoire of teaching strategies. It is important that these conversations are not one-sided – that is, on the teacher's side. If teachers do most of the talking or ask most of the questions then they leave children few opportunities to express their own ideas or raise their own questions. The studies of conversations in the home environment, cited above, reveal that what is characteristic about these conversations is that they are spontaneous and arise from activities in which one or both of the participants are engaged. The conversations are, therefore, given meaning by the context in which they occur.

It may seem to teachers that such learning is not possible in a context where one child shares the attention of their teacher with some 30 or so other children. It is, of course, considerably more difficult to be spontaneous when there is a planned curriculum to follow. However, because time is precious, it is vital that teachers examine the interactions they do have with individual children to assess how much of the characteristics of the successful interactions of the home are mirrored in the classroom. Wells believes that it is neither desirable nor necessary that the style of learning between home and school should significantly change.

> The strategies that children have developed for actively making sense of their experiences have served them well up to this point; they should now be extended and developed, not suppressed by the imposition of routine learning tasks for which they can see neither a purpose nor a connection with what they already know and can do.
>
> (Wells 1985: 68)

Talking to individual children gives the teacher the opportunity to:

- build a relationship;
- know what they understand and think about an activity or experience;
- know what they understand or can do in a certain situation;
- extend their knowledge and understanding through information, suggestion and questioning.

It is this depth of knowledge about a child that enables a teacher to move them through Vygotsky's 'zone of proximal development' (see Chapter 1). Unless teachers know each child's present levels of understanding then they cannot know what their potential might be.

Traditionally, teachers have used questioning as a strategy to discover whether children have either listened to or learnt the information that the teacher has imparted. Many studies of primary classes (for example, Galton *et al.* 1980; Stodolsky *et al.* 1981; French and Maclure 1983) reveal that during interactions with their teachers, children are required to recall a tremendous number of 'facts'. The teacher asks a question to which she or he knows the answer and to which she or he wants children to give a confirmatory response. Questions are not used to enquire into the wide range of understandings that children might hold but to elicit the one particular fact that the teacher wants to confirm. In classrooms, the questions raised by teachers over-whelm – and in some cases completely obliterate – the number raised by children. This is because, by and large, the teacher initiates the topic of conversation and is therefore in control of the ensuing debate. The conversation follows the agenda of the teacher, it is instigated for the purposes of the teacher and the children learn to adopt the passive role of responder rather than sustain their active role of enquirer (Rowland 1984).

When teachers talk to individual children it is important to adopt a style of questioning that extends children's understand-ing and leads them to new ways of thinking for themselves. Questioning that is closed and that requires children to give a correct answer can inhibit the teacher–pupil relationship because children sense that, in a way, the teacher is trying to catch them out. Do they know this, or not? Were they listening, or not? Does this need repeating, or not? Questions that prescribe answers are just as limiting as checklists that prescribe actions. In both cases teachers will only learn what their chosen strategy allows children to reveal. Conversations where the teacher knows the answer and the child does not, establish a power-base for the teacher which inhibits the kind of collaborative construction of meaning that is mutually relevant. It is this willingness on the part of the teacher to negotiate, says Wells, that gives them the confidence to explore their own understandings. Knowledge has to be 'constructed afresh by each individual knower' and teachers cannot rely on the transmission of their own knowledge as a strategy for successful learning by the child (Wells 1986: 116).

Dillon (1981) claims that excessive questioning makes pupils dependent and passive. In order to make effective use of what is at its best a very valuable teaching strategy, it is as well for teachers to be aware of practices that reduce the effectiveness of questioning as a tool in the repertoire of the effective teacher. In their book *Questioning*, Brown and Wragg suggest that the following are common errors in questioning, and their list is useful in raising teacher awareness of their own questioning strategies:

- asking too many questions at once;
- asking a question and answering it yourself;
- asking questions only of the brightest or most likeable;
- asking a difficult question too early;
- asking irrelevant questions;
- always asking the same type of questions;
- not indicating a change in the type of question;
- not using probing questions;
- not correcting wrong answers;
- ignoring answers;
- failing to see the implications of answers;
- failing to build on answers.

(Brown and Wragg 1993: 18)

Talking to individual children is a skilled activity and one that, if the chosen strategies are appropriate, is vital for the teacher's knowledge and understanding of the child and the child's knowledge and understanding of a whole world of things. Questions such as 'what can you see or hear?'; 'what happens if . . . ?'; 'how shall we . . . ?' and 'have you got enough . . . ?' all elicit thinking skills rather than the mere regurgitation of fact.

Talking to the whole class

Early years teachers almost always spend some time in the school day talking to the whole class. These whole class times, or 'carpet' times as they are often called, may be at the start of the day, at lunch time, at the end of the afternoon or before the start of a session. Very often this carpet time will include a 'discussion' about work that has been completed or is about to be undertaken. Discussions such as these are often characterized by teachers eliciting information from children about what they know about or have learnt about a given subject. Research into this kind of dialogue frequently reveals less of a discussion and more of a diatribe. Most of the time, Barnes and his colleagues discovered teachers were retaining the initiative throughout, by a strategy of asking questions and monopolizing the commentary on the answers that were given (Barnes *et al.* 1969). My own classroom research with my colleague Carol Boulter confirms these findings. The infant teachers we observed undertaking different whole class sessions showed these teachers to be concerned with getting the 'right' answer, given by the 'right' child, in the 'right' way.

The 'right' answer

Our video transcripts revealed that 'discussions' were dominated by the teachers' agenda. There was no evidence that they were trying to find out what the children understood as a starting point for the discussions or for planning the future curriculum. They told us they were concerned with finding out what the children had learned from the activities they had set up, rather than finding out what they already knew about and would bring to the experience. They used the technique of questioning to elicit the 'right' answer, that is, the answers that were in their own heads. They did this by rejecting answers that were not those which were deemed to be 'correct'. In doing this they sometimes created conceptual confusion in the children, in that they frequently offered no explanation as to why an answer was accepted or rejected. Therefore children who had been 'guessing the answer in the teacher's head' had no idea why they were either wrong *or* right.

The 'right' child

The teachers further controlled the 'discussions' by insisting that children put their hands up to answer questions. This is common practice of course, but it does give the teacher a controlling mechanism. As classroom gender studies show, teachers use questioning as a way of including and involving miscreant boys – usually sitting at the back of the class – in an attempt to pre-empt antisocial behaviour (see, for example, Stanworth 1981; Spender 1982; Clarricoates 1983). The 'right' child was, therefore, the one named by the teachers, and the naming of the child seemed fairly dependent on one of two factors. Either they were children who were not attending – and, indeed, in every case but one, they were boys; or they were children to whom the teachers turned in exasperation or expectation to give them the 'right' answer – and in *every* case this was a girl.

The 'right' way

In their drive towards the right answer, the teachers were not prepared to be diverted. Consequently if children asked questions or made comments that seemed likely to take them 'off course', they were ignored or rejected. There are different examples, particularly in our transcripts of science lessons, of opportunities to start from the children's concerns or interests being missed. The 'right' way meant keeping to the teachers' agenda, and meeting their intended objectives to cover a certain aspect of the planned curriculum. Such whole class sessions became the expression and exploration not of the children's ideas but of the teacher's. They were in marked contrast to the claims for cognitive development, made by Alexander *et al.* (1992: para. 90) that 'Whole class teaching is associated with higher order questioning, explanations and statements, and these in turn correlate with higher levels of pupil performance'.

Perhaps it is important at this point to remind ourselves that Alexander *et al.*'s discussion paper (*Classroom Organisation and Practice in Primary Schools*) was written primarily about children and their experiences at Key Stage 2. A booklet written in response to this by Tricia David, Audrey Curtis and Iram Siraj-Blatchford (1992) – and dubbed the report of the Three Wise Women – comprehensively dismissed the use of this strategy with nursery and infant children, saying there was inconclusive evidence of its effectiveness and indeed, there was evidence of the *ineffectiveness* of such whole class strategies for the early years (Willes 1983; Stevenson 1987). Nonetheless there are a range of very worthwhile purposes for whole class times (see later in this chapter) not the least of which is the importance of children reviewing with their teacher and with other children what they have experienced and learnt during a session or activity. The introduction of a 'plenary' as part of the literacy hour was recognition of the power of children recalling the range of skills, understandings and attitudes they have rehearsed as a result of both teacher-initiated and child-initiated learning.

According to Tizard and Hughes (1984: 14) school conversations show 'how full of traps the deliberate process of aiding intellectual growth can actually be, and how this process can indeed be counter-productive'. Clearly, if talk between teachers and children is such a critical part of the education process, then teachers must ensure that the strategies they use extend rather than inhibit children's learning.

Box 6.1   Example 5: Planning for talk

A teacher had identified the following learning outcomes for a lesson:

(a) the children will make predictions and justify them;
(b) the children will use appropriate scientific and mathematical vocabulary.

The activity entailed guessing the contents of several birthday presents that had been wrapped in various colourful pieces of birthday wrapping paper. The five 4-year-old children were sitting on the carpet with the presents in a pile in front of them. The activity had tremendous potential. The children were eager to pick up, feel and shake the presents and a lot of valuable language was already being used as the teacher settled down to the activity. Instead of this language being harnessed and extended, the children were told to stop talking. They were then told that they could look but not touch, and the teacher proceeded to lift each present in turn and ask for the children's predictions about its contents, which the teacher recorded. The children were not asked to justify their responses. Indeed any justification . . . 'perhaps you think that because it's hard . . . square . . . noisy . . .' was given by the teacher. By the end of the activity (there were seven presents) the children had made their predictions but not had the opportunity to justify them, even when they had changed their minds following peer pressure. The teacher had used a great deal of mathematical and scientific language, but the children had used virtually none. The worst aspect for the children was that they were told that they would not find out if they were 'right' until the next day . . . when all the other children had done the 'guessing' part of the tasks. This session was an example of the rich potential for language being squandered. The possibilities for use of language were excellent, the children were motivated and the task was highly appropriate. However, the teaching strategies used made all that potential null and void.

Communicating with other children

Children talking with each other to learn is, as we have seen, a relatively new phenomenon in schools. The term 'oracy' was coined in the 1960s by Andrew Wilkinson to stress the importance of the language skills of listening and talking. These separate functions are now enshrined in the National Curriculum as 'speaking and listening' and have been given a new emphasis in the Early Learning Goals within the area of learning entitled 'Communication, Language and Literacy' (QCA/DfEE 2000). Whatever nomenclature is used, oracy now has a distinctive place in the curriculum not only as a medium of learning in all subjects, but as a 'subject' in its own right – as a critical aspect of language competence which is taught alongside the traditionally recognized skills of reading and writing. It is of particular significance for young children for whom 'language plays a part not only in learning self-control but in the formation of conscience' (Pringle 1992: 47). The importance of talk to young children's learning is reflected in one of the 10 aims for the Foundation Stage, that children should have opportunities 'to talk and communicate in a widening range of situations, to respond to adults and to each other, to practise and extend the range of vocabulary and communication skills they use and to listen carefully' (QCA/DfEE 2000: 8).

If children are to have meaningful conversations with each other then they need to be in learning situations that facilitate this. Since the early 1970s, primary school classrooms have generally been organized with children sitting around tables in groups of four to seven (Bealing 1972). The Plowden Report (CACE 1967) is usually seen as having legitimized the move towards a more relaxed classroom atmosphere where children no longer sit in rows waiting passively for the teacher to instruct them. The work of Galton and Williamson (1992) shows that the reasons for the change may have been more complex and varied than simply the desire to promote group teaching and collaborative work, but it is the fostering of collaboration between children that teachers usually give as the prime justification for group seating arrangements.

A number of major studies, however, have highlighted inconsistencies between the way in which children are seated and the tasks in which they are engaged. The ORACLE Project (Galton *et al.* 1980); the Junior School Project (Mortimore *et al.*

1986); Tizard *et al.*'s (1988) research in infant schools; PRISMS (Curriculum Provision in Small Primary Schools) (Galton and Patrick 1990) and the Primary Education in Leeds Project (Alexander 1992) all reveal similar findings – that children may sit in groups around tables, but they are usually working on tasks as individuals.

Grouping children

Grouping as an organizational strategy

Managing large classes calls for creative thinking on the part of the teacher. Even at the level of moving children around the classroom and the school it can be helpful to have children organized in small units. If children are in groups with a collective label such as 'red' group, 'scarf' group or 'leek' group (or any one of the 1001 names that groups are given) some potentially chaotic times such as lining up, getting to assembly and moving round the apparatus can be managed in a more calm and orderly way.

Grouping as an educational strategy

Many teachers feel that children benefit from the sense of belonging to a group, that it gives children security and offers them opportunities to respond collectively and cooperatively. This rationale is essentially social and emotional and does not necessarily fulfil the wider learning needs that the group may have. There is an important difference between children sitting together *in* groups and working together *as* a group. Because research shows that many children sit in groups but work as individuals it suggests that some teachers may group children for the purposes of their own planning rather than the purposes of children's learning. Rather than plan for the individual needs of a class of 30 or more, the teacher plans work for each of, say, four groups and the children are given tasks that are planned for the whole group to do, but which basically require each child to work as an individual. Some typical examples of such tasks would be completing individual maths workbooks, filling in a worksheet or preparing a design for a model.

To maximize the potential of children being grouped together, tasks should require children to collaborate and cooperate. Children who sit together but do not share a common purpose for communication are likely to be distracted by sitting close together (Hastings and Schweiso 1995). This is when talk veers on to topics such as television and pet rabbits. Tasks need to be planned so that children share, discuss, argue, rationalize, find solutions and come to decisions together. If children benefit from speaking when formulating concepts, then it is also vital that they talk with peers who will listen and deliberate their ideas. Thus, if children are to benefit from social interaction, the skills of listening need to be taught alongside the skills of talking. Only if both speaking and listening are a planned part of the curriculum will the social, linguistic and cognitive benefits of group work give an educational rationale for children sitting and working in this context (Box 6.2).

The appropriateness of grouping young children

Putting children in groups in order that they should collaborate is not necessarily appropriate across the full early years age range or in all early years situations. Younger children will not cooperate simply because it is in the teacher's plans. Yet young children will cooperate and collaborate with commitment when they see the need to do so. Observations of young children working on construction or in the home corner reveal just how collaborative they can be, if there is a need. It is important that teachers of our youngest children question the reasoning behind any grouping that is teacher-directed. Is the purpose educational or organizational? Will children benefit from this grouping or is it simply expedient? Will the group aid learning or might it, in fact, hinder it? There is a big difference between being 'put in a group' and working alongside other children. We have already seen how crucial it is for children to work alongside and learn from other children. I am challenging the need for young children to be *put* in a group of children *in order to* work collaboratively. To encourage cooperation between young children, teachers should plan activities and work areas that encourage spontaneous interactive learning opportunities and in which children see a purpose in talking together, working together and learning together.

Box 6.2 A rationale for grouping children

Practical (for the teacher)

- time management;
- ease of planning;
- use of scarce resources.

Developmental (for the child)

social
- recognizing strengths and weaknesses in self and others;
- learning to give and take;
- respecting the opinions of others;
- handling conflict;
- developing management/leadership skills.

linguistic
- communicating for a purpose;
- articulating thoughts, ideas and opinions;
- using different kinds of talk for a purpose.

cognitive
- the development of critical attitudes (to evidence, opinion etc.);
- increase in powers of reasoning;
- opportunities to hypothesize, question and develop ideas collaboratively;
- maximizing thinking power (two heads are better than one);
- the opportunity to go beyond the information given and generate new questions.

Planned grouping

In order to maximize the learning potential of a collaborative activity, the criteria for grouping children need to reflect the purpose of the tasks in which the group are to engage. There are times when it is beneficial for children with similar interests to work together to inspire and motivate each other. There are times when children of similar ability will benefit from the collaborative exploration of a shared challenge. If the choice of group is to reflect the nature and purpose of the task then the implication of this is that groupings will *change* in order for that match to be achieved.

Fixed grouping

Because children have different needs at different times, the teacher has to plan for those needs to be met, not only through the selection of a task, but through the social context in which the task takes place. Grouping that remains fixed and inflexible does not acknowledge the needs of the developing child. Children develop in highly individualistic ways and although patterns of development can be similar, children make spurts and reach plateaux in ways that are highly idiosyncratic. Their development cannot be catered for by decisions about their ability that remain the same for any period of time, particularly if that decision is held as constant across all subject areas or areas of learning. The needs of any small group of children, however similar their ability at any given time, will not be constant from day to day. Because four children are ready to learn about the concept of 'more than' at the same time, it does not necessarily follow that they will come to understand 'the difference between' at the same time. If different rates of learning mean that children have different learning needs *within* one subject, how much more will those needs vary *across* subjects and areas of learning.

Yet sometimes children are grouped with the same children for *all* their learning experiences. Their needs may originally have been assessed in one aspect, such as mathematics, and then presumed to be similar in everything else. How rarely this is the case. Children have such a range of skills and talents and understandings and to suppose that one child can be 'above average' in all curriculum areas while another is consistently 'below average' is to make inaccurate not to mention improbable assessments of children's abilities. Children usually perform according to the expectations of those who influence them. Tell them they're a 'leek' (one of my bright ones) and they'll perform like a leek. Tell them they're a 'cabbage' (my slow learners) and they'll perform like a cabbage, even though some children know that given half a chance they could perform like a leek in PE or technology or scientific investigation.

Labelling children in fixed ability groups can inhibit all manner of opportunities for development. It can restrict the opportunity to shine, gain confidence from and develop in those areas in which the child has strengths. It can also restrict the opportunity to work with a range of peers from whom the child can learn and to whom the child can teach a variety of things. Bringing together children who have the same learning needs at a given time is constructive use of time. Constraining children to work with the same group of children consistently might, at best, inhibit development and at worst can destroy a child's belief in themselves and their ability in anything.

Flexible grouping

Effective grouping recognizes the ever-changing needs of children and the necessity to be flexible in planning the curriculum and the context in which that curriculum takes place. It means that children are brought together because they have similar needs at that moment in time. Knowledge of those needs comes from observations and conversations that identify every child's stage of development and provide clear evidence on which to base diagnostic assessments and future plans. Teachers need to be flexible in their short-term planning so that whatever they discover about children and their development can be incorporated into weekly and daily reviews of every child's needs.

This may sound a tall order, but it is less complex when seen in the light of the fact that – for educational purposes – children do not need to do group work all of the time. If children *sit* in groups but work as individuals then it is irrelevant whether or not they sit at a table with children of the same ability. This kind of grouping is an organizational arrangement and the group may be selected for any number of reasons that may have little to do with the curriculum. There are times when children *need* to work alone and when it is most appropriate that they do so. If, however, the purpose of an activity is that children will learn with and from each other, then it is necessary for the teacher to make decisions about which children should work together to make this an effective learning experience. Children may be set a task to work at as a group, independent of the teacher, or they may be working with the teacher or another adult, addressing a specific learning need. The important point is that the activity is relevant at that time to those children who have been grouped together.

The variabilities of grouping

The groups for which teachers plan can vary in size, composition and permanency. Box 6.3 is a summary of the key issues about the variabilities of grouping.

Box 6.3   The variabilities of grouping

Size

Those who have researched small group work (e.g. Kagan 1988; Fisher 1990) conclude that four children is the optimum group size for effective interaction.

Composition

by age
- often used in vertically grouped classes.

by ability
- children are often selected on ability in language or maths;
- implicit assumption that the child is of same ability across the curriculum;
- implications for teacher expectation and pupil motivation/ performance.

by learning needs
- children brought together with those at similar stage of development in a given area because at that time (for maybe one activity) they have similar learning needs.

by mixed ability
- less able children given ideas and explanations by more able peers;
- more able children given genuine reasons for demonstrating skills and explaining concepts;
- opportunities for children to work with a wide variety of peers.

by friendship
- children motivated by working with those with whom they are happy and confident;
- collaboration most likely to be achieved at first by children working with friends.

The range of learning contexts

Group work is clearly only one context for classroom learning. The teacher has a range of options on which to draw:

- whole class;
- small group plus teacher;
- small group plus another teacher;
- small group minus adult;
- pair with teacher (adult);
- pair without adult;
- individual with adult;
- individual alone.

Given the variety of learning situations in any one class and the variety of needs of the children as learners, how does the teacher make decisions about which context is most appropriate? Alexander *et al.* (1992) state that the criteria should be 'fitness for purpose' and this is a helpful starting point. It seems logical that any decision made in a classroom should serve the purpose of the activity for which it is chosen. However, it begs the question – whose purpose? The choice of social context in a classroom situation may be the child's, but may be – and I suggest more often is – the teacher's. Box 6.4 offers a rationale for choosing different social contexts for learning. The suggestions came from a series of in-service sessions with early years teachers.

The child's choice of grouping

What social contexts would the child choose? Unaware of the myriad of learning opportunities presented by their friends, children work alongside other children for different reasons. Young children learn best in contexts in which they feel secure. Security comes from being familiar with and trusting those who share the learning space. When given the opportunity to work alongside whoever they choose, children do not always work with a special friend. Often their own interest in an activity will determine where they choose to work. Young children do tend to gravitate towards those with whom they are comfortable and confident, however. Being secure enables children to relax, to experiment, to take risks and to stimulate their own learning. Alongside other children they may ask questions or sound out

Box 6.4   Purposes of different learning contexts

Whole class

- telling;
- imparting knowledge;
- enthusing (beginnings);
- sharing (endings).

Small group plus teacher

- differentiation between groups;
- time management (class sizes);
- keeping children on task;
- individualized questioning;
- more opportunities to *listen* to individuals;
- opportunities to observe practical work and social interaction;
- extending knowledge and understanding;
- sharing resources;
- safety.

Small group minus teacher

- revision/rehearsal of the familiar;
- independent discussion;
- collaboration/cooperation (joint outcome).

Pair

- mutual support (response partner);
- shared interest;
- motivation (friendships);
- age – older/younger children supporting.

Individual

- child's need for privacy;
- individual progress;
- pride in ownership;
- maximize concentration.

ideas which, in the company of an adult – however supportive – they may feel inhibited to do. The work of many people who have studied small group work (Barnes and Todd 1977; Jones 1988; Phillips 1988; Reid *et al.* 1989) shows that children are more likely to generate exploratory questions, hypotheses and explanations on their own than when a teacher is present. Working alongside someone with whom you feel secure is a powerful motivating factor. Just think how many adults do not go along to evening classes or join a sports club unless they go with a friend for moral support. Being with someone we like and trust adds to feelings of enjoyment and security and this affects our application to the task in hand.

There are times when teachers want or need children to work with specified others and these pairings or groups may cut across friendships or those with whom the child might instinctively choose to work. Such groupings are valid and valuable. Teachers need children to work together because they are the same or different in their confidence, dominance, gender, ages, ethnicity, language competence or ability. On those occasions when it is possible to enable children to choose their own workmate, however, this enhances children's learning experiences and increases the possibility of sustained interest and involvement in what they are doing.

Grouping children is a complex business. It is an important part of the decision-making processes of the teacher and is concerned with the differentiation of activities. Given the learning needs of the child, with whom should he or she work, and for what purpose? Will the task be best achieved through collaboration? Does the child need the support of an adult? The critical issue is whether the grouping in a classroom is for organizational or educational reasons. It is important that teachers are clear about the two functions of grouping in order that they do not confuse their usage.

Conclusion

Children talk to learn and need to have a range of opportunities to talk purposefully to their peers and to adults. Teachers need to ensure that classroom conversations are not one-sided and that children have genuine opportunities to say what they know and what they feel. When teachers group children for educational reasons, these groupings should be flexible and responsive to the changing needs of children. Young children naturally collaborate and cooperate when they see the need to do so, and they do so particularly when they are engaged in self-initiated activities. The following chapter is concerned with child-initiated learning. It explores the place of play in the early years classroom and asks why teachers can find it hard to justify time for play alongside the rest of the curriculum.

7

THE PLACE OF PLAY

The status of child-initiated experiences

Introduction

No book about early childhood education would be complete without a discussion of the place of play. Any teacher who has been through a training course explicitly designed for the early years will be in no doubt about the place of play in the development of young children's learning. High quality nursery provision has a range of exciting and innovative play opportunities for children as the bedrock of their planned curriculum. Yet this is not usually the case once children enter the world of statutory schooling. Research shows that there is an immense gap between the rhetoric and the reality of play being at the heart of the early years curriculum. While infant teachers quite commonly talk about the value of play, they frequently do not find a place for it in their classroom practice (Pascal 1990; Ofsted 1993b). This book is primarily concerned with teachers trying to implement an appropriate early years curriculum within schools, and so this chapter will focus on the place of play in the early years classroom where the National Curriculum and the Early Learning Goals are all part of the agenda.

A definition of play

Part of the dilemma surrounding play has been that when we speak of it we do not always mean the same thing as the next person. There is no single definition of play and, therefore, playful activities in one form or another have been open to interpretation in different ways. There is however no shortage of definitions and no shortage of writers and practitioners who have put forward a theory of what elements constitute 'play'. For a detailed synopsis of the main theories I can do no better than to refer you to Tina Bruce's book *Time to Play in Early Childhood Education* (1991) and I have used material from this valuable book as the basis for much of the writing in this chapter. Bruce offers a range of examples.

- *Recreation theory*: This theory proposes that play somehow redresses the balance of time spent on work. That play is acknowledged as an appropriate activity for young children but not the same as, and certainly not as important as, work. In this way, play is sometimes used as a reward, as a 'carrot' at the end of a period of work when the child has the opportunity to engage in something of their own choosing once the work for the teacher is finished.
- *Excess energy theory*: Here, play is seen as an acceptable way for children to let off steam and this separates 'worktime' from 'playtime'. This theory has given a framework to the infant school day – and indeed to junior and secondary education too – that has changed little over the years. 'Playtime' is given value in that it releases pent-up energies and prepares children to knuckle down to the more static learning experiences to which they will return.
- *Recapitulation theory*: This theory suggests that play reflects the cultural environment in which the child grows up. Play is seen as being deeply embedded in children's personal experiences and a reflection of the influences of children's environments and the significant people within them.
- *Practice or preparation theory*: Play helps children to prepare for adult life by letting them practise and explore what they need to be able to do as adults. Young children engage in role-play that mimics – often with devastating accuracy – the behaviours of adults who are significant in their lives.
- *Play as pleasure theory*: Play is seen as 'a source of pleasure, and is in no way dependent upon the anticipated results of this activity' (Buhler 1937 in Bruce 1991: 31). This theory emphasizes the importance of play as process, a view strongly held by Bruner (1977: v) who, while not subscribing to the play as pleasure theory, nonetheless asserts that 'Play is an approach to action, not a form of activity'.

- *Affective theories of play*: These are the child-centred theories of play where children are seen as having control over their actions and their lives. There is an important role for others – both adults and children – in acting as catalysts to the play. In these theories, play is seen as continuing into adult life and leading to a range of cultural and creative activity.
- *Cognitive development theories*: These are also child-centred theories but do not stress the importance of play in adult life. Piaget saw play as the means by which the child unifies experience, knowledge and understanding and comes to control them. Piaget saw young children's free play as developing in a linear way into games with rules rather than into more creative aspects of human experience.

Although Bruner's work emphasizes the value of play as process he gives structure to what he constitutes as play, which takes it out of the realms of being a 'free' activity. He sees play as games from the start – games such as peek-a-boo – and sees activities such as sand, clay, water and dough as being without purpose and lacking intellectual challenge (Bruner 1980). Bruner sees the purpose of play as being preparation for adult life, when children take their place in society.

Vygotsky (1966: 6) sees play as both cognitive and affective, referring to it as 'the leading source of development in pre-school years'. Like Piaget, he sees play as having rules, not ones that are formulated in advance, but ones stemming from the situation itself. Because of this Vygotsky discounts the notion of play as pleasure, citing the playing of sporting games, which are 'very often accompanied by a keen sense of displeasure'.

- *An integrating mechanism*: Tina Bruce has championed a more precise definition of play. Building on the work of Froebel, McMillan and Isaacs, she develops the notion of 'free-flow' play. This process is 'concerned with the way children integrate, use and apply their knowledge'. In *Time to Play* (1991: 57), Bruce outlines 12 features of free-flow play which help to clarify its definition and help to tease out 'how free-flow play differs from struggle, exploration and practice, or from representation, games and humour':

1 It is an active process without a product.
2 It is intrinsically motivated.
3 It exerts no external pressure to conform to rules, pressures, goals, tasks or definite direction.

4 It is about possible, alternative worlds, which involve 'supposing', and 'as if', which lift players to their highest levels of functioning. This involves being imaginative, creative, original and innovative.

5 It is about participants wallowing in ideas, feelings and relationships. It involves reflecting on and becoming aware of what we know, or 'metacognition'.

6 It actively uses previous firsthand experiences, including struggle, manipulation, exploration, discovery and practice.

7 It is sustained, and when in full flow, helps us to function in advance of what we can actually do in our real lives.

8 During free-flow play, we use the technical prowess, mastery and competence we have previously developed, and so can be in control.

9 It can be initiated by a child or an adult, but if by an adult he/she must pay particular attention to features 3, 5 and 11.

10 It can be solitary.

11 It can be in partnerships, or groups of adults and/or children who will be sensitive to each other.

12 It is an integrating mechanism, which brings together everything we learn, know, feel and understand.

(Bruce 1991: 59–60)

The importance of play

I have noted just a few of the many claims made for the importance of play, yet play still has to fight to maintain its place in many early classrooms. One reason may be the undermining of confidence caused by claims that much of the theorizing about the importance of play has been carried out in the absence of any real evidence that play does or does not have the effect and benefits postulated (Smith and Cowie 1991). Bruner (1966), despite his own stance on play as 'practice in mastery' and his belief that being playful is a time when children learn to take important risks and find boundaries as well as freedoms, still wrote of the 'extraordinary dogmatism' that play is beneficial to young children. This view is what Sutton-Smith and Kelly-Byrne (1984) have called the 'idealization' of play. Much of the work of the 'early pioneers' of early childhood education (as Bruce refers to them) such as Froebel (1782–1852), McMillan (1860–1931) and Isaacs (1885–1948) can be seen influencing the practice in play environments in nurseries and schools in Britain today (see Moyles 1989; Bruce 1991; Smith and Cowie 1991) but their work was based largely on first-hand and anecdotal evidence rather than the kind of 'hard' evidence which is required by formal research methodology.

This situation has been addressed more recently, however. The Froebel Blockplay Project (see Gura 1992) was an empirical study of children's play and play behaviours in which researchers analysed the development of children's blockplay as an integral part of the whole curriculum. Those engaged in the project analysed the development of play at the microlevel and examined the use children made of play to represent some ideas more powerfully than through words. It is a study that demonstrates the crucial role of adults in play and the roles that adults can adopt as researchers as well as practitioners. A second important study was funded by the ESRC at Exeter University (Bennet *et al.* 1997: x) and explored reception teachers' theories of play, aiming to 'provide a more secure foundation for play in the curriculum by challenging entrenchment, assumptions, polarized views and vague terminology'.

One possible reason why play does not hold its place in the early years classroom is because teachers do not have, or make, the time to gather the kind of observations that would give them the evidence they personally need to be convinced of the importance of play. Let us look at this issue in relation to some of the early theories.

Recreation theory

In the play as recreation theory, play has a different status from work. It does not have the status reflected in Vygotsky's view that 'a child's greatest achievements are possibly in play' (1966: 92). The status it is given places it firmly in second place to work. Work is more important because it is controlled by the teacher and must usually be completed before – as some kind of reward – children are allowed to play. This time to play is very often referred to as 'choosing' and this term also signifies the status of the play. It says to children that there are only certain, very limited, times when they have control over their learning experiences and can exercise choice and make decisions. The rest of the time children's experiences are in the control of the teacher and are dominated by the teacher's choices and her or his decisions. The reasons for play being relegated to this position are twofold. The first must be that the teacher actually *does* see play as being less important than work. If she or he did not, then play would have a different status and a different place in the classroom experience. The argument that there is not time for play shows that play is not seen as *process*, a way of integrating or consolidating skills and understandings, but as a separate activity, another subject to be added on to all the other subjects that have to be covered.

The second reason for play being relegated in the classroom hierarchy is that play motivates and interests and absorbs children and is ideal for using as a 'carrot' in order to encourage children to finish the possibly less inspiring and motivating tasks set by the teacher. It is also valuable in keeping children out of the teacher's hair while she or he completes the designated teaching tasks. In this way, children get further messages about the place of play. Not only is it something that is less important than work, but it is also something that the teacher is not particularly interested in because she or he spends more time working alongside children engaged in tasks that she has initiated. Play is consigned to the corners of the classroom – both in terms of time and space. It is not observed by the teacher, who rarely finds time to participate, in play. Resources are limited and space for play is cramped because space for work has higher precedence. Time for play is dependent upon the amount of time in any session before play, PE, television or whichever interruption to the day is next on the timetable. No wonder children come to view play as being subsidiary to work.

Indeed they also seem to learn very quickly once they enter school that if it is play it cannot be work. Fein (1981) found that children between the ages of 5 and 9 have very clear ideas about work and play, which can only have been formed from their own experiences. Work is compulsory, done for an adult and is very often done alone. It is subject to judgement and evaluation by others, and has performance criteria – usually right or wrong. Play on the other hand, is voluntary, it is done for its own sake, often in company with others, and is subject to judgement by the child. Adelman (1992: 139) sees this division between work and play as part of the influence of the Protestant work ethic in schooling where play is seen as 'a temporary and privileged release from the hard grind of real work, study and training'.

Whatever its genesis, the ethic is alive and well and living in classrooms.

Excess energy theory

Children are active learners and the most appropriate curriculum for them is one that offers experiences which involve them in investigation, exploration and play. What an indictment then for the infant curriculum, that children need to let off steam. It suggests that children have been passively engaged rather than actively involved, required to sit and listen more than move and do. It is interesting to consider that a 4-year-old in a nursery does not need a playtime, but it is deemed that the 4-year-old in the reception class often does. As we saw in Chapter 5, the development of an outdoor area for learning was seen as an antidote to the passive learning environments so indicative of classrooms at the turn of the century. A properly designed outdoor environment offers children the chance to engage in a whole range of active learning situations, including the many opportunities to develop their physical skills through climbing, rolling, throwing, cycling, pushing and so on. This is not 'letting off steam'. It is a crucial part of educating the whole child, an acknowledgement that physical development cannot be separated from the development of the mind and the emotions. When children work in the outdoor area this is not a time for teachers to sit back and take a supervisory role. It is a time when adults are engaged as much as children, supporting and guiding children's experiences in the same many and varied ways as they do indoors.

The lack of outdoor provision for children in infant classes is well documented. There has been a substantial increase over the years in the number of 4-year-olds in primary schools, frequently working in classes alongside children of 5, 6 and 7 years of age. Studies that have examined the quality of provision for these young children reveal many situations where standards are low and quality is almost non-existent (see Sestini 1987; Thomas 1987; Pascal and Ghaye 1988; Bennett and Kell 1989; Brown and Cleave 1990). The most frequent omission in this provision is that of a properly fenced off, appropriately equipped outside area. It is easy to see why. Outdoor equipment, especially large apparatus with proper surfacing, is not cheap, but there is so much more that could be done to develop the outdoor learning environment for young children which would give them opportunities to play outdoors in constructive, developmental ways (see Chapter 3), and not simply in order to release excess energy.

The most recent *Curriculum Guidance for the Foundations Stage* (QCA/DfEE 2000) makes many references to the importance of outdoor learning experiences for young children from age 3 to the end of the reception year. It is to be hoped that as schools plan and budget for the addition of outdoor areas of learning for their reception age children that the benefits of learning out of doors will become apparent for children throughout their primary schooling.

In the meantime, primary schools should at the very least address the quality of the play experiences children have at playtimes in order to make them more positive than they currently are. In *The Excellence of Play* (1994), edited by Janet Moyles, David Brown writes a very helpful chapter examining the playground as a context for children's learning. He claims that 'Play areas provide a setting for a cultural forum within which the children can create and recreate meaning from the sum of their experiences' (1994: 64). Brown reminds us that the opportunities children have for playing together in groups with their peers have declined considerably and that the playground has become all the more important as a context for the learning of certain sorts of behaviours.

Recapitulation theory

The quality and nature of children's play is highly culturally specific. The value and status given, or not given, to play in classrooms is often a reflection of the culture of the school community or the teacher's own cultural conditioning, which cannot accept that if an activity is playful it can also be worthwhile. Janet Moyles in her book *Just Playing?* explores the different perceptions of parents, teachers and children towards play activities and concludes that 'Whatever the difficulties faced by all parties, the child needs the kind of concordance and co-operation that real partnership with parents requires, particularly in relation to the value attached to the child's play' (1989: 164).

In *The Excellence of Play* (Moyles 1994) Audrey Curtis examines in greater depth the value of play in different cultures. She describes an investigation into the use of the microcomputer in the nursery classroom and found that parents from Asian cultures

---

Box 7.1   Example 6: Improving provision at playtime

One school has made a great and effective effort to improve the quality of the children's playtime experiences. The headteacher and staff believed that not only did the children need more quality time but that it would also encourage adults – teachers, classroom assistants and dinner supervisors – to see their role in this context as going beyond a supervisory one.

The adults first learnt and then introduced to the children many old rhymes and playground ditties that have gradually disappeared from children's experience. Because of diminished opportunities to play together, most of these childhood rhymes and songs were unknown to many children. The school population has children from diverse cultural backgrounds and the songs and rhymes from each of these cultures were unfamiliar to other children, and experiences needed to be shared.

Some children did not want to spend playtime rushing around getting hot and said they would prefer to sit and talk, or engage in activities such as reading, mark-making or construction, so these were provided. Other children wanted to be more active but not necessarily play football. The use of footballs was curtailed on a rota basis and a whole variety of small apparatus such as hoops, ropes, quoits and bean bags were introduced instead. Because of the interaction by the adults these did not simply disappear – as had apparently happened on previous occasions – but are used constructively and with clear enjoyment and enthusiasm by children of all ages.

The behaviour of the children has improved dramatically. Many more children can engage in purposeful activities at playtime and the relationship between children and the lunchtime supervisors has improved. Not only have these improvements altered the quality of playtimes, but teachers report an improvement in behaviour throughout the rest of the day.

---

were particularly enthusiastic about its use 'as they frequently have difficulties in accepting the traditional nursery-school curriculum with its opportunities for freedom of choice (1994: 33). Few western parents, she continues, will admit to giving their children specific toys for pure fun, although she quotes a delightful comment made by an African mother to Rabain-Jamin (1989: 298) who claims 'We give toys [to children] to play with. You give them toys to teach, for the future. We feel that children learn better when they are older'.

Whatever views parents hold, it is the responsibility of teachers to explain and exemplify the value of play in the classroom. At the same time, teachers will always need to be sensitive to the experiences of children and the culture from which they come, not only in order to understand the values and expectations that children may hold but also to resource the play environment with materials and equipment that will be of value and meaning to children and their everyday lives.

Practice or preparation theory

There are many ways in which young children practice 'being an adult'. Part of this is an exploration of the roles of people whom they know and love. Part of it is being intrigued by what it might be like to be a grown-up. Part of it is acting out real experiences and assigning themselves roles in order to play out a situation. According to Garvey (1977: 88), some of this kind of play represents 'only salient events in a sequence of action . . . Most enactments are clearly created from concepts of appropriate behaviour and are most likely not direct imitations of people'.

A home corner that changes to an office or hospital or shop or dentist's surgery or bank or submarine, or any of the countless innovative ideas that can be seen in classrooms, should be a constant source of opportunity for children to engage in activity which they perceive prepares them for adult life. The joy of this kind of dramatic play is the fusion of fantasy and reality, of being able to deal with issues in a context that enables children to risk the exploration of a whole range of personal and relevant experiences.

Play as pleasure theory

Most definitions of play will include some statement about the necessity for the activity to be pleasurable. In a survey of play literature in 1983, Rubin, Fein and Vandenburg distinguish play through six criteria, the first of which is that play is 'intrinsically motivated'. This would suggest that the child finds it pleasurable enough to want to do it. Bruce's use of the delicious word 'wallow' in her free-flow 'equation' (1991: 42) also signals activity that is giving someone a great deal of pleasure. Janet Moyles claims that 'Play has its own intrinsic rewards, it is done spontaneously and voluntarily and it is thoroughly enjoyable' (1989: 133), while even the Department for Education and Science (as it then was) makes the statement that:

> Play that is well planned and pleasurable helps children to think, to increase their understanding and to improve their language competence ... Teachers know that such experience is important in catching and sustaining children's interests and motivating their learning as individuals and in co-operation with others.
>
> (DES 1989: para. 16)

Affective theories of play

It is the control that children have over play activities which makes them pleasurable, particularly in school. So much of a child's day is spent responding to the direction of the teacher that engaging in play allows children to regain the learning initiative. Vicky Hurst (in Moyles 1994) asserts that children's play links with the ways in which all humans, adults as well, come to make personal sense of the world. This is a profoundly controlling state in which to be and gives us some sense of why good quality play experiences have such an impact on the learning and lives of young children.

Affective theories of play emphasize the importance of the role of others – both adults and children – in acting as catalysts to play. The Froebel Blockplay Project recorded a wealth of valuable examples of ways in which children and adults support and extend each others' play ideas. Their research proposal (Gura 1992) aimed to look at three different roles which might be adopted by adults in their support of play. These were:

- *laissez-faire*, i.e. children are often left to use the blocks without adults;
- *didactic*, i.e. where tasks are frequently set by adults and adults dominate play interaction;
- *interactionist*, i.e. where adults help and encourage play with an emphasis on adult–child play partnering; in order to do this 'adults need to know as much as possible about the

development of young children, and the context of learning' (Gura 1992: 20).

The laissez-faire approach, they conclude, 'tends to leave children where they are'. The didactic approach encourages 'dependency, narrowness, a desire to please those in authority, conformity and a lack of creativity, imagination or the ability to create and solve problems'. The interactionist approach 'begins where children are, helping them to use what they know, and to move with them into new knowledge and understanding'. One fascinating finding of the project was that children adopt the adult model of interaction in adult-absent situations with peers. This, they conclude, implies that adults need to *organize* to be absent (as opposed to doing this by default), as well as to be present.

'Structured' play

There is a significant difference between being a catalyst for an activity and dominating it. The time and place for adult intervention is a finely judged thing. Intervention at the wrong moment can be interference, and all practitioners know that terrible feeling when a wrongly timed question or comment can bring some freely flowing play to an abrupt halt. In the need to justify play as a worthwhile *school* experience, some writers and practitioners have suggested that the involvement of adults gives weight and credence to a pursuit that would otherwise be too frivolous to take up valuable time.

In drawing a distinction between play that is child-initiated and play that is initiated by the teacher, Manning and Sharp (1977) used the phrases 'structured' and 'unstructured' play. This is an unfortunate differential in that it suggests that child-initiated play lacks structure. Even more unfortunate is the assumption that unstructured play is somehow the next step to structured play, that children progress from one to the other, that when they are bored with lack of structure the teacher saves the day by injecting some.

To begin with the notion of a linear progression in play is inappropriate. Young children need activity that they initiate to be happening alongside, betwixt and between activity that is initiated by adults. Adults have a crucial role in supporting and extending play, but there is a fine line between intervention and interference. The minute an adult has a predetermined task or goal in mind, then the activity cannot be play. It becomes, in my own nomenclature, a *teacher-initiated* activity (see Chapter 4), along with any task for which a teacher has planned predetermined ends. To conclude, we should remember that in the words of Susan Isaacs (1968: 133) 'play has the greatest value for the young child when it is really free and his [*sic*] own'.

The rhetoric and the reality

I want to return now to the 'often enormous' gap identified by Chris Pascal in her (1990) study of infant classrooms and reiterated by Bennett *et al.* (1997), between the principles about play which teachers espoused and the reality of practice in their classrooms. In Pascal's study, while 82 per cent of teachers expressed free/imaginative play as their first curriculum priority in providing a curriculum for the 4-year-olds in their class, in practice they employed a greater number of teacher-directed strategies and were 'less comfortable' with child directed strategies. The study by Bennett *et al.* (1997: 17) found that teachers had 'significant problems relating to the nature and purposes of play in educational settings' and claimed that 'relying on a disparate ideological underpinning to justify play is insufficient since this has failed to provide a unified theoretical and pedagogical knowledge base to guide practice'.

Perhaps the inclusion of a substantial section on play in the *Curriculum Guidance for the Foundation Stage* (QCA/DfEE 2000) will help practitioners confront their principles and their practices around play and help restore it to a central place within the early learning environment. There is currently a real issue about addressing practitioners' 'pedagogical knowledge base'. Since the late 1980s, play and child development have been squeezed out of initial teacher training programmes in favour of a more subject-based approach. This has resulted in many new teachers having little or no understanding of the pedagogy of play and how to integrate play into planning for learning. There is an urgent job to be done by all Early Years Development and Childcare Partnerships in implementing a programme of professional development around play. If play is to be 'a key way in which young children learn with enjoyment and challenge' (QCA/DfEE 2000: 25) then early years practitioners must be more knowledgeable about its purposes and how it relates to the more formal teaching practices to which many teachers still adhere. Any old play will not do. If play continues to be a carrot for when work is finished, or only takes place in cramped corners with poor equipment, or is never observed by adults and adults never intervene, then it will continue to be part of the rhetoric and not the reality of children's experiences.

This situation is not new. The investigation into the experiences of 4-year-olds in school by Bennet and Kell (1989) found that only 6 per cent of time was spent in play, while Tizard *et al.* (1988) estimated that top infants in the inner London schools she and her colleagues observed engaged in play for less than 2 per cent of their time. The situation does seem to have worsened as the number of 4-year-olds in school has increased. In 1993, the Office for Standards in Education completed a survey of 88 English primary schools to inspect the work of 141 reception classes. They reinforced many of the points raised by Pascal's study:

- rarely were schools able to make good provision for outdoor play (para. 16).
- lack of space sometimes meant that access was restricted to other valuable learning activities, for example sand and water (para. 16).
- when the lessons were at their best, the adults [demonstrated] ... their ability to sustain and extend talk and play (para. 22).
- The quality of learning through play presented rather a dismal picture. Fewer than half of the teachers fully exploited the educational potential of play. In more than a third of schools play was only recreational; it lacked an educational purpose and was usually undertaken only after work had been completed. It was largely ignored by adults but sometimes regarded as a useful time filler when pupils were tiring of the main work. In the poorer classes teachers over-directed work and under-directed play. They used play as a reward for finishing work or as an occupational or holding device. By contrast, in the effective classes play was used positively to develop children's abilities across a wide range of activities. For example, the provision of 'home corners', sand and water play activities which are long standing features of the work with young children were planned into the programme with a sound educational purpose rather than as time fillers (Ofsted 1993b: para. 25).

I make no apology for including paragraph 25 in its entirety. In the light of all that has been said in this chapter, we must address how teachers in the 'effective' classes were able to 'use play positively to develop children's abilities across a wide range of activities'.

Play and the external agendas

The place of play has been threatened by the introduction of the National Curriculum and, more recently, the literacy and numeracy strategies. This needs to be confronted. First, there is nothing in the National Curriculum documentation that explicitly negates, undermines or refutes the value of play in early childhood education. There are, in fact, a number of examples within the programmes of study that positively encourage play as a process of learning (EYCG 1998). The argument from teachers is usually one of time. Because there is so much to cover then there isn't time for play. Now is the time to reiterate what has been said earlier. To suggest that there is insufficient time for play intimates that play is something extra. It is not. Play is a key process whereby children will gain their knowledge and understanding of science, maths, history and any other of the National Curriculum subjects. The quality of the learning experiences if play is of high quality should be all the greater. If time is finite – as we discovered space to be – then once again priorities have to be established and teachers must use their professional judgement in deciding which activities will most enhance young children's learning. If we cannot do it all, then what is best for children? There is sufficient evidence to suggest that the learning opportunities offered through play make it a classroom imperative.

The literacy strategy in particular challenges the place of play because it advocates an hour of adult-directed learning. Even within the 'group and independent work' where children still need a balance between adult-initiated and child-initiated learning, it is difficult for them to have control over their experiences and activity. Many literacy advisers and consultants encourage the use of play equipment, space and resources – particularly imaginative play – as an integral part of the repertoire of literacy hour experiences. More often than not, however, the adult has clear learning intentions in mind, for example re-enacting the story of Goldilocks and the Three Bears, and as we saw earlier, this negates the experience being 'play' in its free-flow sense. Nevertheless, there are increasingly optimistic signs that the rigid application of the literacy hour is being relaxed, particularly for younger children. There is an understanding that for young learners, recorded language and literacy activities often make them very dependent on an adult and therefore it is not good classroom practice to give a whole class a range of activities that mean that large numbers of children will be reliant on an adult for support at any one time (see Chapter 4). Of equal importance is that if children engage in play that is meaningful, worthwhile and driven by their own interests and needs, then they cannot help but engage in communication and language. Blockplay, creative exploration, role-play, experiments in sand and water all give rise to a wealth of opportunities for speaking and listening and the imaginative area introduces children to writing for real purposes. There is a place for play in the literacy hour in just the same way as there is in an integrated day. The triangle model in Figure 4.1 is every bit as appropriate and necessary in planning for an effective literacy hour as it is in any other early years situation. Perhaps, as we have seen, there is an even greater need for child-initiated learning in the literacy hour, First because the agenda is so teacher-dominated, and second because so many of the activities need to be supported by the teacher and, as we have already seen, the teacher can and should only plan to be in one place at any one time. Most important of all is the recognition within the *Curriculum Guidance for the Foundation Stage* (QCA/ DfEE 2000) that the introduction of the literacy hour itself should be delayed until Year 1. There is a world of difference between an hour of literacy and a literacy hour. A high quality early years curriculum will provide more than an hour of literacy. The literacy strategy objectives will be best met by a more flexible, loosely structured model of classroom management in the early years.

Raising the status of play

In order to raise the status of play in classrooms, teachers need to have first-hand experience of its value. They need to make a commitment to it as central to the curriculum for young learners. Box 7.2 suggests a charter for play that may support practitioners

---

Box 7.2   A charter for play

1 *Acknowledge* its unique contribution as a process by which young children learn.
2 *Plan* for it as an integral part of the curriculum and not an 'added extra'.
3 *Facilitate* it with appropriate and high quality provision.
4 *Act* as a catalyst when intervention is appropriate and a scaffolder when expertise is required.
5 *Observe* it in order to have first-hand evidence of children's learning.
6 *Evaluate* it in order to better understand the needs of the learner.
7 *Value* it through comment and commitment in order for its status in the classroom to be appreciated.
8 *Fight* for it with rigorous, professional argument in order to bring about deeper understanding and acceptance by colleagues, parents, governors and the community at large.

---

and their managers in raising the status of play in early years classrooms.

Conclusion

Play is the natural way in which children go about the business of learning. It enables them to integrate and consolidate a wealth of experiences that enhance their cognitive, physical, social and emotional development. It naturally encourages cooperation and collaboration, requires the use of fine and gross motor skills and demands cognitive application. It is pleasurable, but also helps children face pain and sorrow. It is consuming and challenging and motivating. The relevance of play to early years education is unquestionable and its status in the classroom should be assured. In Chapter 8, we look at other situations in which children can have power and control in classrooms and see whether children can be motivated by the negotiation of elements of their learning and their learning environment.

8

THE NEGOTIATED CLASSROOM

Issues of power and control

Introduction

The idea of learning being negotiated is a challenge to any curriculum that prescribes the process and content of experiences without taking into account the current needs and interests of children. A developmentally appropriate curriculum, as described in Chapter 3, is built on what individual children know and need to know next. It is a curriculum that starts from the child rather than expecting the child to start from the curriculum. It presupposes that children are aware of the purpose of the activities in which they are engaged and are able to make judgements about their value. When teachers see the desirability of motivating children in this way, then the learner is placed in a powerful position. Rather than being a passive recipient of someone else's decision-making and control, the learner is an active participant in the formation of their own classroom experiences. When young children exercise control in classroom situations it determines the relationship between teacher and learner. The relationship becomes a partnership in which children can negotiate input and outcomes in ways that increase their autonomy and sense of purpose. This does not diminish the role of the teacher but alters it. The idea that learning is controlled by the learner

presupposes that knowledge is not transmitted directly from the teacher to the learner. It demands that both teacher and learner recognise that the subject matter of learning resides outside their 'circle of intimacy', rather than exclusively in the teacher.

(Rowland 1984: 149)

Being a pupil

Within the first few hours of being in school for the first time, or being in a new class, a young child picks up messages about their role in the classroom and what it is like to have collected their first title in life outside the culturally secure daughter, son, granddaughter, nephew. This title 'pupil' carries with it attitudes and expectations, now their own, but learnt from the attitudes and expectations of those around them. 'When you're at school you won't be able to do that'; 'at big school they keep you in at dinnertime if you haven't finished your work'; 'now you're at school you'll learn proper things like sums and writing' – a mass of expectations that usually come in the form of well meaning advice, but can also carry the undertones of threat.

In this way, children arrive at school with a notion, correct to a lesser or greater extent, about what it means to be a pupil. Children believe they are in school to learn and the teacher to teach. The active role is that of the teacher and the appropriate role for a pupil is to be passive and receive the teaching. Children frequently adopt a role that is quite different from the natural role of competent learner that they have played so successfully in the home. This suggests that children often do not make a link between their learning behaviours in the home and their learning behaviours in school. Why should this be? Perhaps it is because they are simply not given opportunities to engage in these activities often enough to see school as an extension of their previous learning environment. Or perhaps the mere fact that they have to come to a different, separate place to 'learn' implicitly suggests that this was not what they were doing before. Acknowledging the young child as a competent learner means making the early days as smooth a transition from home to school as possible. It also means sending messages to the child that what they are and what they bring with them by way of knowledge and experiences is of value and will affect their classroom life. If children are cut off from their previous success and expected to behave in ways that are alien to them then this can exacerbate the myth that being a *pupil* is different from being a *child*.

Changing a child into a pupil

When children arrive at school there are batteries of experiences that are designed to change them into pupils. The first of these is often the learning of school routines. These are patterns of behaviour that are designed by teachers and learnt by pupils through the imitation of older pupils or through the understanding of teacher cues. The exhortation to 'wait here for the present' (Lee 1959) is well known and loved, but there are ranges of other demands made of children that can leave them equally bemused. One child was told to 'Go and put those on your peg' and turned to his mum and said miserably, 'But I haven't washed them'. Teachers do not intentionally mislead, but children are being required to absorb a new vocabulary and a series of behaviours at a time when many are at their most vulnerable, having left their parent or carer, maybe for a whole day, maybe for the first time.

For many children this is also their first experience of being one amongst many, the first time they may have had to share the time and attention of adults, and this can be difficult. Just when you need someone to reassure you about a whole host of things that are new and bewildering, you cannot find anyone who has the time. Then when you want to say something – when there is an adult, a 'teacher', sitting close by within asking distance – you meet the most entrenched routine of all . . . putting your hand up. Sinclair and Coulthard (1975) call this 'bidding', which is an excellent description. The child is bidding for the teacher's time by raising her or his hand in response to the demand to do so. It is a request to hold the floor and have the teacher's attention. Putting up your hand demands an understanding of two basic rules: one, that in order to speak to the teacher, this is what you need to do; two, that there are times when you can talk to other children and times when you cannot, and this is one when you cannot unless you are told you can, in which case you must but only when you're told!

Because the rules and routines are bewildering, many children resort to imitation. Sometimes that imitation is of other children who have been in the class longer or who have simply cottoned on faster. Children offer responses 'that clearly enough imitate those that have recently been offered and have seemed to please the teacher well enough to get positive feedback' (Willes 1983: 186). Sometimes the imitation is of the teachers who, as Mary

Willes describes, through their 'intonation, gestures and expression' give out clues which the child is left to guess about and test the meanings.

The rules and routines are frequently non-negotiable. They are the prerogative of the teacher, and often she does not choose to or think to divulge them. Thus becoming a pupil is seen by Willes as learning these teacher initiatives as rapidly as possible:

> The minimal, inescapable requirement that a child must meet if he [sic] is to function as a participating pupil is not very extensive. It is necessary to accept adult direction, to know that you say nothing at all unless the teacher indicates that you may, to know that when your turn is indicated you must use whatever clues you can find, and make the best guess you can. There are prerequisites to learning this. It is necessary to want adult attention and approval, and to be able to attend to a person or to a topic for more than a moment or two.
>
> (1983: 83)

This is 'training' in the true sense of the word. It is learning to respond in a given way to a given signal – behaviour with Pavlovian overtones.

Pleasing adults

The notion of pleasing adults is a very important one in the discussion about power and control in classrooms. Holt (1982: 70) suggests that 'it is only when pleasing adults becomes important that the sharp line between success and failure appears'. This implies that children's perceptions of their own success or failure, their own worth and value come from the values and perceptions of the teacher. We know that there is evidence of a self-fulfilling prophecy that operates in classrooms. Tell a child that they are good, will succeed, are doing well and the child obliges by responding with enthusiasm and proving you right. Tell a child that they are worthless, useless, hopeless or any other damning adjective directed at a certain group of children daily in their school lives, and lo and behold they prove us right again. Holt suggests that being incompetent has two advantages: first, it reduces what others expect of you and second, it reduces what you expect or even hope of yourself. When you set out to fail, he says, one thing is certain – you cannot be disappointed.

Chapter 1 showed that, whatever their experiences, most young children arrive at school as enthusiastic and energetic learners. Their early experience at school can bring about a transformation in their attitudes and behaviours so that they become a shadow of their former competent selves. Such are the expectations of schooling that being a pupil for some children can mean doing what the teacher says and conforming to what the school demands. Howard Gardner, in his powerful book *The Unschooled Mind*, suggests that somehow

the natural, universal, or intuitive learning that takes place in one's home or immediate surroundings during the first years of life seems of an entirely different order from the school learning that is now required throughout the literate world.

(1993: 2)

In similar vein, Janet Meighan (1993: 43) suggests that once children begin school, 'Learning how to learn gives way to learning how to be taught'.

So we return to the main question of this book. Why, when children in their early, formative years have achieved what Gardner calls a 'breathtaking array of competences with little formal tutelage' do some of those same children suddenly become dependent, passive learners, reliant on the teacher for success and self-esteem? Gardner (1993: 3) suggests that 'schools were instituted precisely to inculcate those skills and conceptions that, whilst desirable, are not so readily and naturally learned as [their] intuitive capacities'. There is more than an element of truth in this. Schools are devices of society and therefore must respond to the requirements of that society and of the cultures it serves. Unfortunately, in fulfiling this requirement schooling can denude children of all their inherent powers as learners and make them feel as though their needs and their interests no longer have a place. For some children, the transition from home to school marks a transition from success as a learner to failure. All too often it is the child who is a truly intuitive learner who is at greatest risk. Schools do not often cater for individuals. Because of their very nature they demand a good deal of conformity, and schools that are not sufficiently flexible to allow for the idiosyncrasies of learners are likely to alienate some of the most creative and free-thinking children.

Disaffected learners

Feelings of alienation come about when there is a mismatch between the child's expectations of the school and the school's expectations of the child. According to Willes (1983), some pupils apparently step out of line because they do not know where the line is drawn. Some children, however – those who are already having feelings of alienation because they do not fit with the school's expectations of a pupil – know where the lines are drawn, but deliberately cross them. In the introduction to her book on disaffection in the early years, Gill Barrett defines disaffection thus:

> Fundamentally the word implies a negative state of something that was once positive. Thus affection for something has been reversed to become disaffection. Here we are concerned with disaffection in the early years of schooling. Thus, instead of affection for the activities of schooling, disaffection implies a dislike and hence a turning away from the activities and learning expectations of the classroom and school.
>
> (1989: xiv)

If one considers that some children have only just started school, the implication of this definition is that the 'affection' was for learning that happened in contexts prior to and outside school. Disaffection therefore comes hard on the heels of affection for situations in which the child saw him or herself as competent. Running right through this book is the notion of the young child as both a competent and motivated learner, and it is a dreadful indictment of the institution of school which can turn that motivation and competence so quickly into disaffection.

The need to be seen as a learner

We have seen how important it is for children's existing competences and their previous experiences to be seen as valuable and of intrinsic importance to any future learning and development. Children who have strong feelings of self-worth, the basis for most successful learning, are those who know their contribution to be welcomed and their experiences to be valued. Neville Jones, in his preface to Gill Barrett's book, suggests that 'By definition, disaffected pupils invariably feel in some respect devalued persons' (1989: xii). When self-esteem is eroded then children begin to exhibit the kinds of behaviours that show an alienation to the culture of school and the expectations of the classroom. In an occasional paper written for the Council for Educational Technology in 1987, the writer W.J.K. Davies explores different views of what learner autonomy might mean, both in theory and practice. He suggests that it is essential that learners are confident in being able to handle the learning they perceive they need, otherwise they become confused and frustrated, and disillusionment creeps in. He offers evidence that when adults were invited to initiate learning, their learning needs were rarely what had been anticipated. Even their starting points and learning sequence through a given piece of content often differed widely from what the tutor considered logical. If this is true for adults and their tutors, then how much more relevant is it to children and their teachers?

Disaffection in older children

When children are older then they behave, says Neville Jones, in ways that 'have a tendency to exacerbate their feelings of disaffection' (in Barrett 1989: xi). So with children, particularly of secondary age, we may see disruption, vandalism, maladjustment, absenteeism and truancy. These 'active' forms of behaviour cause many problems for teachers while pupils are in school. There is another form of disaffection however, the passive form, which is 'possibly more insidious' (Jones in Barrett 1989). Pupils simply opt out of ordinary school activities but in ways that mean that sometimes the teacher does not notice. This disaffection can have implications beyond school life and 'maybe throughout the life of the pupil'. The new agendas for active citizenship and life long learning should address some of these major concerns in more systematic ways (Huskins 1998).

Disaffection in young children

Younger children are much less likely to turn to the kind of active behaviours described above, so how does their disaffection manifest itself when they have feelings of low esteem and frustration? They are unlikely to withdraw themselves from the environment, as most young children choose to remain within the security of the school even when feeling very aggrieved.

Their most likely response is to reject or withdraw from the activities or tasks they are being required to perform. If this withdrawal is 'active' the children can throw tantrums, disappear under tables or absent themselves into another room of the school. Barrett (1989: 30) claims that

> school, with all its new expectations and people, is likely to provoke strong responses such as crying, hitting other children and removing oneself from the source of frustration. If the child knows that these strong responses have always been responded to by an adult in the past, and the cause of frustration removed and dealt with, then it may cause even stronger response behaviour in school when the initial crying or attempted withdrawal fails to remove the expectation.

This is a terrible picture of the distress that some children feel and the anger they consequently display. If the rebellion is more passive, then children simply stop doing what is asked of them, do it extremely slowly or make sure they disrupt as many other children as possible in the process.

There can be no doubt that disaffection arises because children are asked to do things at school that make little sense to them. It is no justification to say that children have to learn to do this in life and therefore they should start now. This rationale is used for an astonishing range of experiences, from sitting still during registration to enduring competition in games. Children may have to face a myriad of unpleasant and unhappy experiences before they grow old and die but this is no justification for inflicting such experiences on children just so they can practise their future unhappiness.

One of the greatest frustrations for young children is that often they cannot articulate their own feelings. They find it hard to explain or describe what they feel and why. Gill Barrett's important study shows that if teachers are patient enough to ask – and willing to find out the answers – to why children are not responding positively, then they are half-way to resolving the problem for the child and, of course, for themselves and the rest of the class.

A further frustration for young children is the amount of interruption they get from teachers when they are engaged in activities. We have seen that one important principle of early childhood education is that the young learner has time for periods of sustained activity. Whether this is initiated by the child or the teacher, an adherence to the principle is crucial if children's experiences of learning at school are to emulate their experiences at home and if the teacher is to give positive messages about the worth of the activity in which the child is engaged. Barrett gives examples of the intense frustration young children feel when their experiences are interrupted:

> Daniel and Carl have found a book on New Zealand (Carl's homeland). They start to read when the teacher calls, 'Time to put them away'. Daniel's face and comment show disappointment. 'But I've only just got it.'
> There are always too many people in school to take things properly. You have to stop too soon. Someone always spoils it.
>
> (1989: 10)

Many teachers and whole school staffs are addressing the issue of interruptions to the school day. Research by Campbell and Neill (1990) confirmed what all teachers know, that there is insufficient time in the school day for all that has to be done. An audit of how time is spent in school can reveal how much learning time is fragmented by the school timetable. Assemblies, playtime, lunches, television and so on, all interrupt the flow of learning for children. Each break requires teachers and children to wind themselves down and then to wind themselves back up again to achieve the momentum that was stopped. This is not an efficient use of time and it is a useful exercise to examine the interruptions in a classroom or within the school, and see if there are ways in which such interruptions can be minimized.

The negotiated classroom

School, as we have seen, is a place where rules and expectations are frequently governed by adults and where children are unable to stake a claim. It is usually adults who create the learning environment for children, but what happens if teachers consciously and deliberately give children a stake in the process? What is possible if, in order to maintain and sustain their motivation, application and *rights*, children are taken on as partners in the shared negotiation of practice and behaviour?

The notion of negotiation

Sylvia Warham (1993: 35–6) suggests that in some ways teaching and learning are in themselves a negotiation because 'the process requires the consent of both the teacher and the learner'. The negotiation of the learning context between the teacher and the children is a negotiation of what the children will allow the teacher to do and what the teacher will allow the children to do. Successful negotiation requires messages to emanate from the teacher. When children are listened to and their ideas and interests absorbed into the fabric of their curriculum experiences then this is a positive starting point for the negotiation of the more complex elements of classroom life.

Teacher identity

There is a whole range of classroom issues that can be negotiated with children. The extent to which these are adopted in classrooms depends very much on the style of the teacher and her or his personal identity. Warham (1993) identifies teachers who have 'dominant identities' and those who have 'less dominant identities'. She suggests that teachers who have dominant identities in the classroom situation 'created inequality. The children found that only one person at a time could be dominant and they had to compete with one another and the teacher if they wanted to take part in the [class] discussion' (Warham 1993: 35–6). On the other hand, the less dominant teachers appear to have 'no control over the situation', but in fact use a far greater range of strategies in interaction with children than the dominant teachers. By encouraging children to be independent thinkers and learners, the control that less dominant teachers exercise is far more subtle, but far more effective. Effective teachers, says Warham, adopt both dominant and less dominant strategies in different situations, but she warns that it is important to be conscious of the positive effects of habitually less dominant strategies which, she claims

- foster trust, confidence and security;
- encourage in children a sense of self-worth and respect for others;
- encourage independence and self-reliance;
- encourage children to develop their own initiatives; and foster a sense of equality.

(Warham 1993: 37)

While habitually dominant power strategies may not prevent children from learning, it is possible they carry with them certain inherent risks. Warham suggests that it is possible they may

- foster competition to the point of confrontation;
- damage group and individual relationships;
- discourage the children from taking initiatives;
- make the children dependent upon their teacher; and risk damaging the child's future attitude towards teachers and education.

(Warham 1993: 37)

The notion of negotiation can only sit comfortably with the less dominant teacher strategies described above. The remainder of this chapter is devoted to looking at ways in which teachers can move towards the kind of classroom that acknowledges children's competences, respects their rights as individuals and sees education as a collaborative venture between learners.

The negotiated classroom

The possibilities for negotiation within classrooms fall into three broad categories:

- *organization*: when and how it is to be learnt;
- *context*: where and with whom it is to be learnt;
- *curriculum*: what is to be learnt.

Organization

The start of the day

At the beginning of the day children are full of energy and, we hope, enthusiasm. If they arrive at school and are required to sit down, sit still and – probably – sit quietly, then immediately they are having to adopt behaviours that suit the purposes of the teacher rather than themselves. The children's needs are subsumed beneath the needs of the teacher to sort out the early morning problems, to juggle children and parents, and to be seen as having a calm, controlled class. The beginning of the day does indeed establish the tone for much that will follow. If the day begins in ways that repress children, for whatever purposes, then it sends negative messages to children about those in power and control in the classroom, and in some children can set up feelings of frustration, alienation and resentment before the day has hardly begun.

In some classrooms, on arrival at school, children get straight down to activities that they choose themselves. Parents are encouraged to stay for as long as they can or want, and while children are engaged independently or with their parents or carers, the teacher can get on with her administration or organization in the knowledge that the children are working purposefully. Some teachers are concerned about starting the day in this way because of their responsibilities over completion of the register. However, completion of the register does not rely on children sitting on the carpet and responding to their names. In nurseries children rarely meet on the carpet for registration and yet nursery teachers too need to know how many children are in school at any time. Nurseries have a whole range of strategies for recording the arrival of children, from hanging names on a 'tree', to posting names in a letter box. In some classes children write their names on a blackboard or whiteboard when they arrive. There are a whole variety of strategies that teachers can employ if they feel that a formal registration does not set the tone they want for the start of the day.

The organization of the room

When I was in my first year of teaching I used to spend days before the beginning of each term organizing my classroom. I drove the caretaker mad by arranging and rearranging my classroom. I made labels, signs and charts, spent a fortune on card and pens and tacky-backed *everything*. I believed that it was part of my professional responsibility to make the room as 'ready' for the children as I could, so that it would look like a ready and welcoming environment in which we could all get down to work. As I began to give more and more time and thought to the involvement of children in decision-making processes within the classroom, however, I realized just what wonderful learning opportunities I was taking out of the hands of the children. Real life problem-solving situations frequently stare us in the face in classrooms, and instead of responding to them as heaven-sent opportunities, we subject children to the contortions of 'identifying a need' for a problem for which they will rarely realize a solution and which they would never in a million years have identified for themselves.

Classrooms *need* organizing, however. As Chapter 5 describes, there are decisions about space and resources that are fundamental to the establishment of an environment that is conducive to independent learning. Since this is an environment in which children are to learn then it seems entirely logical that it should be an environment that they help to create. Once I realized this I left the furniture where the caretaker had left it – in a heap in the middle of the classroom (yes, that really *was* his practice!). Then when the children arrived, we worked together to decide what learning areas were needed and where resources should go. Then came the business of sorting, locating and labelling resources which, because the children were so involved, gave them a sense of ownership over the classroom that they never had when I made the decisions and took the action, when they were not around.

Discipline: rules and sanctions

One successful way of helping children to respect and adhere to rules and sanctions is not to impose them from on high, but to negotiate them. Children can become involved in establishing rules that they perceive to be necessary in order for their classroom to run smoothly and for the benefit of all. Children's rules sometimes reveal interesting insights into their perceptions of what is or is not important and what is or is not likely to happen in classrooms. 'The children mustn't spit' said one 4-year-old, recently arrived at school – now where did *that* idea come from?

The sanctions that children work out for themselves can be very enlightening. I had endeavoured, as a headteacher, to alter my role within the school in the disciplining of children. Rather than seeing children only when they had been naughty, I asked the staff to send me children with whom I could share something positive and worthwhile. This seemed to be working well, so I was dismayed when the reception class, on negotiating their own sanctions, ended a long list of mounting retribution with 'No. 6: Send them to Miss Fisher for telling off.' Children's perceptions are not altered overnight.

If rules make sense to children and if sanctions seem appropriate, even if not necessarily 'fair' in adult terms, then children are more likely to feel a sense of responsibility in maintaining them.

One last word about rules, and that is – it is best to keep them positive. It contributes so much more constructively to the ethos of the classroom if the list talks about what we *will* do and be like, rather than what we must *not* do or be like.

Order of work

Negotiation of the order in which children do their work is bound up with decisions about the amount of control we believe children should have over their learning experiences. Chapter 9 sets out various ways of encouraging children to be independent in their movement from one activity to the next. Inherent in this independence is the control that comes with being able to organize work in the order in which it suits the child. Chapter 2 talked about children being 'larks' and 'owls' just as adults are, and if we are to get the best from children then they must be allowed to plan the ebb and flow of their working day as it suits them.

The introduction of the literacy and numeracy strategies in England has challenged the amount of freedom teachers feel they can give children to plan their own work and timetable. Many schools are now organized so that literacy and numeracy teaching are whole school slots before and after break. Consequently, the free flow of children from one activity to another, from adult-initiated to child-initiated learning, has become much more difficult to manage. As has been previously discussed in Chapter 7, guidance on the implementation of the literacy and numeracy strategies has become increasingly responsive to the needs of the youngest learners. The *Curriculum Guidance for the Foundation Stage* (QCA/DfEE 2000: 27) says that 'Reception teachers may choose to cover the elements of the literacy hour and daily mathematics lesson across the day rather than in a single unit of time.' The guidance for Ofsted inspectors (2000: 13) clearly states that, in the Foundation Stage, it is

> up to teachers to use their professional judgement and know-
> ledge of the needs of the children in their class when decid-
> ing the most appropriate way to manage the introduction of
> [the literacy and numeracy strategies].

Letting children negotiate the order of their work presupposes an element of trust between teacher and child that work will be completed (see Chapter 9), but this is all part of the negotiation process. If children know that they are being trusted and are being given the opportunity to make their own choices and decisions then they also know, because it is a part of the 'negotiation' made explicit by the teacher, that they have to fulfil their side of the bargain. Negotiation can never be one-sided and a classroom where children do their own thing, but not the teacher's, is not a negotiated classroom. Part of the developing relationship between the teacher and the class must include discussions about what choice and decision-making means, and it includes the responsibility to fulfil all sides of the bargain and to complete the tasks that the teacher initiates as well as the tasks children want to initiate themselves. On the teacher's side, the bargain is that she or he does not set up so many teacher activities that the time for child-initiated activity is squeezed out. Planning is critical. If time has been allowed for a balance of activities (see Chapters 4 and 9), then it is perfectly appropriate for a teacher to remind a child that there is only x amount of time now in the day/week and there is still y to be completed. Most children, given the self-respect that comes from making their own decisions, respect in turn their teachers and will complete what is outstanding – even if reluctantly at times. In negotiated classrooms where children can choose the order in which they do their work there is a purposeful and dynamic atmosphere. It is rare to see the persuasion and coercion that can go on in classrooms where children are required to complete successive tasks set by the teacher with no room for negotiation or using their initiative.

Length of time on work

When children can negotiate the order in which they do their work then it is implicit that they will be able to determine how long they will spend on a task. Time management is something that many adults could usefully learn, but even young children can develop this skill when given experiences that leave decisions in their hands. Most children learn to pace themselves given sufficient experience of having control over time and their own learning activities.

As we have seen earlier in this chapter, children need sustained periods of time in order to produce work of quality and depth (EYCG 1992). It is up to the teacher to plan for the delicate balance between sufficient time being given to the needs of the child and sufficient time being given to the demands of the external agenda. Some teachers worry about the child who, despite reminders or help with time management, still works all day on a child-initiated activity, for example, the sand tray. If there are a lot of interesting and absorbing activities in the class then most children want to experience more than one thing in any one day. However, if a child is genuinely reluctant to move and clearly is gaining something valuable from their self-selected activity then what is this telling us about the child? If teachers see children's behaviour as a learning opportunity for themselves, then this may be a way of reducing the amount of confrontations that can dog classroom practice. Children who need to repeat experiences may be in need of reassurance of something familiar. They may be feeling unsettled or unwell and simply find the repetition of something they know offers them the security they temporarily need. If the behaviour is out of character and continues, then this should alert the teacher to investigate reasons for the child's behaviour. Forcing children simply leads to alienation. It may bring about a temporary result, but will not enhance the children's attitudes or approaches to learning. As Holt says, 'If the situations, the materials, the problems before a child do not interest him [sic], his attention will slip off to what does interest him, and no amount of exhortation or threats will bring it back' (1982: 265). Children can be trusted to set their own pace. They will need opportunities from the teacher to manage and organize their time, but as with all elements of independent learning, this is time well spent.

Context

Place of work

Where we work can have a significant bearing on our application to a task. I am sure I am not alone in feeling that I cannot do my own writing unless I am in the relative tranquillity of my study, and cannot settle to read the Sunday papers unless I have my legs up on the sofa and the cat on my lap. Locations can promote or inhibit learning and, as with everything else, what is desirable for one person can be thoroughly undesirable for someone else. If a classroom is designed along the lines of the 'workshop' approach outlined in Chapter 5, then children will already have the freedom to move around the room in order to find resources and use equipment. However this freedom is fettered if children are then required to go back to a predetermined place to complete the task in hand. If a child truly concentrates best sitting alone, lying on the floor, working with a friend, then the classroom should be arranged so that this can happen. Part of negotiation is being able to justify a decision made (on the part of the teacher as well as the children) therefore a child who chooses an unusual work location may be required to justify it to his or her peers and the teacher. If the quality of everyone's work is not compromised then the decision is justified. If work is adversely affected, then the teacher and other children are at liberty to challenge the decision and suggest a different one.

Sometimes, in classes where children are getting used to their independence, there can be children who seem to be 'flitting' – to be going from place to place without settling for long, or who go and watch other children without actually joining in themselves. This situation is another learning opportunity for the teacher. Children who flit fall generally into two categories. There are those who are unsure of themselves and need to see the range of what is possible but do not yet have the confidence to try something for themselves. In this case flitting is very valuable because it means that the child comes to gain confidence through observations and imitation and almost always joins in once this is achieved. Then there are children who need supporting towards independence. Perhaps they are given little independence at home, are used to having things done for them and need support to make decisions for themselves. In this case the teacher needs to make it part of her or his 'teaching' (or perhaps that of the classroom assistant) that the child is helped in small stages to begin to make decisions and to act on their own initiative. One of the most important parts of this is to gain the understanding of parents so that they extend independence to the child's life at home.

With whom to work

Most of us work better when we work alongside people whom we like and whom we trust. You only have to try and separate teacher colleagues at in-service training courses to realize just how strong are our adult feelings of security in people we know! If children are not in fixed groups then for most of the day they should be able to work alongside those with whom they want to work. If they are working on a task as an individual then it makes no odds whether they are sitting next to somebody doing a different sort of work. There will be times when the teacher wants certain children to work with others (see Chapter 6). However, for the remainder of the time, young children do not collaborate readily unless they see the need to do so, in which case they organize themselves very effectively. So being able to work with someone you choose to work with usually gives children an added sense of motivation. Of course there are some exceptions to this. Once again it is part of the negotiation process. If children do not work in cooperative and constructive ways with the person or people whom they have chosen, then the rest of the class and/or the teacher can suggest alternative ways of working.

The curriculum

The topic

In Chapter 3, I expressed certain reservations about topic work, in that it can be hijacked by teachers and have little relevance to the class or individual. If choices of topic are not made too early then the interests of children can be incorporated. If at the long- and medium-term stages the subject concepts, skills and knowledge are identified then it can be left to the individual teacher and their class as to how these are brought together and integrated. An individual teacher can be given the identical set of concepts and skills as a colleague in the next class, but given their knowledge of the particular needs and interests of their own class may choose to plan for and integrate these elements in quite a different way to the other teacher. Negotiation with children encourages teachers to consult children as much as possible and to amend their planning to take account of children's opinions as much as is possible.

The key questions within a topic

One very successful way of involving children in the overview of their work is to brainstorm with them all the things that they would like to find out about the topic that they are to follow. By raising questions, children come to see that the work they are doing and will be doing has the express purpose of answering these questions. One enterprising class I know writes their questions on huge pieces of card and suspends them from the classroom ceiling so that everyone is reminded that these are the points that are to be investigated. In this way the teacher is seen as learner alongside the children and the emphasis is on the process of discovery rather than the transmission of facts.

When children have ownership of their learning in this way there are far more opportunities for them to use their initiative both at school and at home to come up with answers or pose more questions of their own.

Criteria for success

One of the ways in which teachers display control in the classroom is by being in charge of what is deemed to be good, appropriate or sufficient with regard to children's work. Children come to rely on their teacher's judgements for affirmation and approval and do not believe that their own opinion matters. Teachers use words like good, well done, brilliant and so on, they draw smiley faces and award stickers. All of these mechanisms say to the child that it is what the teacher thinks that matters here. Judgements about value and worth are by the teacher's criteria. When children are reliant on the teacher's evaluations in this way they are usually left in no uncertain terms about whether the teacher is pleased or not.

Very often, however, they can be left bemused as to *why* this work was 'fine' and this 'not your best'. In an interesting article called 'In praise of praising less' (1991), the author Mark Tompkins warns against empty praise. The article suggests that the teachers should give their *opinions* rather than their *judgements* and make specific reference to the details of the child's activity or the process the child has used. If children have negotiated the purpose of the work and understand why they are doing what they are doing then they are far more likely to be able to give a rationale for when something has been undertaken or achieved to their own satisfaction. In some classes I know, teachers negotiate with children the 'success criteria' *before* an activity begins. In other words, they ask 'What do you think will make this a successful model plane?' 'What do you think would make this discussion effective?' 'What will make this an interesting story for the readers in Class 4?'

When children are clear about success criteria – where this is appropriate to an activity – then it helps give them a clear framework in which to work. These practices have been mirrored in the introduction of individual target setting with children. This initiative builds on what is seen as effective practice in encouraging children to articulate what they are good at, where they need to improve and what help they need to do so. This is a powerful and constructive use of self-assessment which, if implemented with sensitivity, should enhance children's self-awareness and increase their self-esteem.

Audience/use for finished work

Sometimes children are pleased with their efforts and want to share what they have done. Sometimes they are dissatisfied and want to start again. Sometimes they are dissatisfied and want to do something else. If children make a decision that their work is not acceptable to them then usually they should be at liberty to dispense with it as they choose. Some children screw work up because they are so lacking in self-esteem that they cannot believe they have achieved anything of worth. Whatever the reason for satisfaction or dissatisfaction, choosing what happens to a piece of work should be the child's decision. Yet so often that piece of work automatically becomes the property of the teacher. 'I just want to borrow it for the colour display'; 'you can take it home at the end of term'; 'mummy will be so pleased to see it on the wall'. The 'I just want to borrow this for the wall/portfolio/class book' puts the teacher firmly back in control of what happens to children and their work. There are legitimate reasons for teachers wanting children's work for display. These should be explained to the children. If children then decide to do something for the display in the hall then that is their choice. If they do not, then that is also their choice and tells us something, perhaps, about the relevance of the hall display to that child.

Planning the day's work

This aspect will be covered in depth in Chapter 9. Suffice to say here that if children are to have a sense of ownership of their learning and their learning environment then negotiating their day's work must clearly be part of this. An element of self-selected activity is crucial – not just in terms of motivation but in terms of giving status to a critical element of young children's learning. Children need to be able to negotiate much of what they do, the order in which they do it, the time they spend on it and with whom they do it. Box 8.1 summarizes what and when children can negotiate.

Box 8.1   The negotiated classroom

Long- and medium-term planning

- Long- and medium-term planning identifies the concepts, skills, knowledge and attitudes within each subject that the teacher plans to introduce, revisit, develop over a given period of time.
- The activities identified at this stage should be *possibilities* only.

Short-term planning

- Short-term planning takes account of the needs and interests of a specific class of individuals.
- Teacher-initiated activities and child-initiated activities should be happening alongside each other.

The teacher observes and has conversations

- What can the child tell me about himself/herself as a learner?
- What does each child already know/understand?
- What strategies/skills does each child use?
- How does each child work with others?
- What is the child interested in?

Teacher plans

- What does the child need to know now? (concepts/skills/ knowledge/attitudes)
- How is this best learnt? (differentiation=activity/ process/outcome/grouping etc.)
- What support does the child need?
- How can I include the spontaneous interests of children? (and who shall give it?)

Child plans

- What work do I want to do today?
- What work do I need to do today?
- In what order shall I do my work?
- Where shall I work?
- With whom shall I work?
- What resources/ equipment do I need?
- What do I want to do with my finished work?

Teacher plans (continued)

- Which activity will be teacher-intensive?
- Are the other activities planned so that the children can be independent learners?
- What kind of support/ intervention do the other activities need?
- Have I planned to revise both teacher-initiated and child-initiated activities?

The teacher observes and has conversations

- Have I planned to observe teacher-intensive, teacher-defined *and* child-initiated activities?
- Have I planned to involve the child in *self*-assessment?
- What is the focus of my assessment of the teacher-intensive task?
- Will I observe or participate?
- Have I identified the evidence on which to base my assessments?
- What strategies have I established for recording unplanned observations/conversations?
- How will I use all the evidence collected to inform future planning?

Conclusion

If children are to emulate their early success as learners once they start school, then teachers need to ensure that there is not a great gulf between being a child and being a pupil. Children who are expected to behave in ways that are alien and irrelevant to them may become disaffected as learners and this disaffection frequently occurs when children have no control over their own experiences in school. When teachers are committed to a learning partnership with their pupils, then there are many ways in which children can negotiate learning. The power and control this negotiation gives children can be a powerful and motivating force for learning and is likely to lead to positive, life-long atti-tudes towards learning and accomplishment (Schweinhart *et al.* 1993). Some teachers believe that giving children control means that they themselves will lose it. My experience is that this could not be further from the truth. One reception teacher who evolved a negotiated classroom with her children remarked, 'The more control I give away, the more in control I am'. The next chapter draws together the many practical aspects of previous chapters in suggesting how children can be helped to organize their own learning experiences.

9

PLANNING, DOING AND REVIEWING

Children organizing their learning

Introduction

This chapter looks in practical ways at how young children can organize their own learning. Previous chapters have suggested that in a well-organized classroom, where space is utilized effectively and where children can find and replace their own resources (see Chapter 5), children can work with increasing independence. The role of the teacher is crucial in planning classroom activities that take account of the considerable amount of time that young children spend working alone. The planning of activities needs to acknowledge the difference between the kind of activities that children undertake alongside an adult (teacher-intensive activities) and the kind that are successfully tackled alone (teacher-initiated activities; Chapter 4). The order in which work is done and those with whom work is done are also features of a negotiated classroom (Chapter 8) and each of these different features contributes towards children's increasing autonomy as learners. This chapter is concerned with how children can organize their own learning, how they move independently from one activity to the next and how their independence is supported in constructive and purposeful ways.

There are a number of strategies that teachers use to support children's independence and to encourage their self-discipline and sense of responsibility. One such strategy involves children in having considerable responsibility in planning their own learning in some of the ways described in Chapter 8. This strategy aims to motivate children by giving them opportunities to make choices and decisions in doing their work. It makes explicit their own responsibility in seeing an activity through by including regular opportunities for reviewing and evaluating their achievements.

Planning

> Children who are able to plan for themselves see that they can make things happen. Children begin to view themselves as people who can decide and who can *act* on their own decisions; they have some control over their own activities.
>
> (Hohmann *et al.* 1979: 62)

In classrooms where all children do the same activity for a pre-scribed period of time there is little scope for children to plan, because their work and the order in which they do it is dictated by the teacher. However when teachers plan for a range of tasks to be happening at any one time and children move to the next activity when they have successfully completed the previous one (rather than everyone moving on together), then children have opportunities to have some control over what they do and when they do it.

Children need to plan for both teacher-initiated and child-initiated activities, just as teachers need to provide both (see Chapter 3). They can decide which activity to begin with and which to do next and so on. Young children may only manage to plan their initial activity. Older children will, in time, be able to plan their whole day (or two days, or week) all at the same time. It is important that children know what activities the teacher has initiated and the time scale for their completion. Some teachers plan a day at a time; some give children two days to complete a set of activities and in some schools even the youngest children are given their tasks for the week and plan their time accordingly.

In order to keep the balance of classroom activities (Chapter 4) and for all activities to have equal status (Chapters 7 and 8) children need to be able to move freely from teacher-initiated to child-initiated experiences. They need to find the ebb and flow of their own day by organizing their time to match their energy levels and interest levels. This does not open the doors to chil-dren to play all the time and not work at teacher-initiated tasks. The purpose of negotiation is to accommodate the demands of others and this frequently requires compromise. Children come to understand that part of having the freedom to make choices is the necessity to accommodate teacher-initiated tasks alongside those that they initiate for themselves. My experience of observing classrooms where children have these opportunities is that the delineation between the teacher's work and their own becomes blurred. Children see all activities as being a relevant part of their schoolday and work at them all with a purpose.

As long as teacher-initiated activities are completed by the time the teacher has specified, then children can start with either a teacher-initiated activity or a child-initiated activity and proceed in any order they choose. In this way children have a substantial degree of control over their learning and are motivated by the decisions they are able to make. Having this kind of control encourages children to demonstrate growing autonomy as they come to learn that they are accountable for their planning and their action (see reviewing, pp. 162–9).

Oral planning

In the early stages, planning will be verbal. Children identify what they are going to do and then go and do it. For younger children, the teacher may gather together a range of resources and materials to act as prompts for the variety of activities on offer. This is a good strategy for reminding all children about what is available in the classroom and for drawing their attention to activities or equipment that is not being regularly used.

When children plan verbally, it is necessary for the teacher to record their plans. In this way the teacher has a record of the range and balance of activities which children choose over a period of time and also a ready reference point for when children review their work later in the day. If children do not complete the tasks they have planned then this can tell the teacher a lot about the child's level of maturity and whether or not the process of planning and then doing is understood. Being able to *plan*, *do* and then ultimately *review* is a sophisticated process and children need time and support if they are to understand the cycle as a whole.

Recording planning

Once children are able to record their own plans then there are a number of ways in which these can be represented. Children can circle an object that is representative of the activity they are going to go to; draw a freehand picture; draw and write the word or draw a symbol for the table or area in which they are going to work. The recorded plan helps children to develop their capacity to express their intentions in increasingly complex ways and acts as a personal prompt when children come to reflect on their work later in the day. At every stage it must be down to each child to plan in a way that is useful and relevant for him or her. The system should be highly flexible and accommodate as many different ways of planning as there are children.

Doing

> Work time is a time for adults to observe and learn what interests children and how they perceive and solve problems, to take cues from children and work along with them and to support, encourage and extend children's ideas.
>
> (Hohmann *et al.* 1979: 72)

In order to be able to go off and work independently, whether on a teacher-initiated activity or a child-initiated activity, the classroom has to be appropriately planned (see Chapter 5). Young children need constant reminding about where everything is and their responsibility for putting things back when they have finished with them. Children who are used to managing themselves and working independently will be able to settle quickly to their activities. Some will be returning to activities that they have left on the previous day, some will be starting activities that they will initiate and some will begin with tasks that the teacher has initiated.

The order of activities

In classes where children are given the chance to organize their day's work in their own way they have come up with the following options:

- doing all the teacher-initiated work first and then initiating their own activities afterwards;
- doing all the child-initiated work first until reminded by the teacher that the negotiation in this classroom means that the

teacher-initiated activities need to be started *very soon* or else time will run out;
- doing activities alternately, first a teacher-initiated then a child-initiated.

Some teachers are concerned that unless they direct the order of work, children will arrive at the same activity or area at the same time, and there will be insufficient space or resources to accommodate them. Such situations are, in fact, a critical part of the problem-solving day for independent learners. Initially the teacher asks 'what do you think you can do about this (problem)?' The children then realize they can go on to another activity and come back to this one later. In time, children will not need to ask the teacher 'what shall I do?' but will go through the problem-solving process independently.

Once children are engaged in their independent activities then the teacher can begin their own teacher-intensive tasks and have time and space to work with their chosen group(s) in a focused and profitable way.

Working alongside other children

Chapter 6 discussed the business of grouping and whether and when it is an appropriate strategy to employ with young children. Planning a day that suits the child as an individual presupposes that children are not always working in a predetermined group unless they are brought together by the teacher for a teacher-intensive activity or they are working with other children on a collaborative task. Bringing children together to work as a group when they are chiefly working as individuals can cut across the organization of the class. It is difficult for children who are already involved in something to be told to leave it so that they can go and work with particular children on a particular task. This is not likely to bring about instant cooperation. Most teachers who have grappled with this issue have decided that the best solution is to begin group work after there has been a break in the children's work for another reason – such as PE, playtime or assembly.

Interruptions to the school day

This brings me to the number of interruptions in the school day which conspire to stop children from working. Predetermined arrangements such as those mentioned above militate against the sustained periods of concentration, which are such an important element in children's learning. The Curriculum Guidance for the Foundation Stage (QCA/DfEE 2000: 11) reminds us that 'Children need time to become engrossed, work in depth and complete activities' – both those 'planned by adults and those that they plan or initiated themselves'. People who say that young children have short concentration spans are giving them the wrong things to do. Anyone who regularly observes young children will have seen the total absorption and perseverance they demonstrate when engaged in an activity that interests and challenges them. Such activities can have been initiated by the teacher or by the child. When children rush teacher-initiated activities it is frequently because they have not understood the purpose of the activity and are completing it for the teacher rather than for themselves.

Once children begin statutory schooling the interruptions to their day multiply alarmingly. Some of these interruptions are understandable. If there is only one hall between eight classes then the space needs to be timetabled and everyone needs to keep to their allotted times. But what about playtimes? Why do we insist on children going out to play all at the same time just because it is an established pattern of the school day (see recreational theory of play in Chapter 7)? Many children have only just settled from assembly or a hall time, or are deeply involved in their activities when they are made to stop and play on demand. Any adult who has control over their own patterns of living, be they work or social, knows that you take a break when you *need* to take a break, when your body tells you that you are ready for a change of scene, or pace or activity. The break is then truly beneficial and gives fresh impetus to the next phase of concentrated activity. This is why a permanent outdoor environment, appropriately resourced and staffed, is the most beneficial answer to this problem. Given such a resource children can follow the ebb and flow of their work patterns outside as well as in. Children have increased opportunities for using gross motor movement and exercising their bodies energetically. Given that most schools are not fortunate enough to have such a resource for their 4-year-olds, however, let alone their 7-year-olds, how can this issue be addressed? Most schools have now abolished afternoon playtime. Teachers often feel that the disruption to both the working afternoon and the children's behaviour is not conducive to a calm end to the day. In the morning, however, playtime is still a feature. In one school I know the teachers decided that they could be more responsive to the class (if not to individual children) if each class took morning break when that class needed it, rather than all together at a prescribed time. For some classes, on some days, this meant not taking a break at all because children were absorbed in their work, but for most classes it meant taking a break when children's concentration and application were on the wane and once the learning opportunities of the session had been optimized. The difficulty with this arrangement is organizing a break for teachers and giving them the opportunity to do all those things that make breaktime so valuable to them. The logistics of this would need to be worked out by individual staffs and there would need to be universal commitment to the notion of a staggered playtime. However, where schools have good classroom support, it is possible to organize a shift system – as they do in nurseries – to enable each adult to get a break. As playtime is a time when children are often interrupted, in their work and their behaviour, then teachers may want to consider this option.

The role of the adult

The role of the adult in the process of planning, doing and reviewing is critical. As we have seen in Chapters 2 and 6, active learning is a social, interactive process and it is essential that all adults foster a climate that is supportive of this. Chapter 4 examines the role of the teacher in detail, but I like the summary in the High/Scope handbook *Educating Young Children* (Hohmann and Weikart 1995: 50–1) which identifies the effects of a supportive climate on both children and adults:

- children and adults are free to learn;
- children gain experience in forming positive relationships;
- adults see children's behaviours in terms of development;
- children grow in their capacity to trust, be autonomous, take initiative, and feel both empathy and self-confidence.

Hohmann and Weikart (1995: 52) go on to outline five key strategies for creating supportive climates:

- sharing of control between adults and children;
- focusing on children's strengths;

- forming authentic relationships with children;
- making a commitment to supporting children's play;
- adopting a problem-solving approach to social conflict.

The role of all the adults in the life of the child are emphasized and the High/Scope approach highlights the necessity of patterns of behaviour being established both at home and school, so that children benefit from the mutual involvement of their families and their teachers (further details of the High/Scope approach will be obtained by reference to the handbook).

Completing tasks: what to do with finished work

In an independent classroom, children need to move from one activity to another without recourse to the teacher. Of course it would be ideal if every child could have a response to every piece of work immediately, but if we are looking at the realistic use of limited teacher time, then I do not believe this is possible without the teacher's focused work being constantly interrupted. This is another compromise situation and because of the realities of classroom life I would suggest that there are some activities that need an instant response from the teacher and some that just have to wait for one.

If an activity does not require an instant response, what do children do when they have finished the task? If the task is child-initiated then the child may choose to do one of several things:

- clear away and move on . . . the process has been more important than the product;
- put the outcome of their endeavours somewhere in the class where it will be safe – a specially located shelf, tray or surface;
- put the outcome somewhere where the teacher and/or other adult will be able to see it when they are ready – perhaps a small table by the teacher's chair;
- take the outcome or the 'story' of the process to the teacher for an instant response.

If the task is teacher-initiated the child may choose to do any of the following things:

- clear away and move on if the task has been concerned with process and not product (an investigation rather than a problem to be solved);

- put the outcome of their endeavours somewhere in the class where it will be safe – a specially located shelf, tray or surface;
- put the outcome somewhere where the teacher and/or other children will be able to see it when they are ready – perhaps a small table by the teacher's chair;
- take the outcome or the 'story' of the process to the teacher for an instant response.

Whichever they choose, children's independence and their willingness not to interrupt the teacher will rest on their knowledge that the teacher *will* share their work – if the child wants the teacher to – within a relatively short space of time from its completion. This is one important reason for having a regular review time and we will move onto this a little later in the chapter.

Completing tasks: how do I know they'll do it properly?

One question I am often asked is, if children move from one activity to the next without recourse to the teacher, how do teachers know that they will have done their work 'properly'? There are several issues here. First, teachers know their classes well and very quickly make judgements about those children who usually apply themselves and those who may need a little extra encouragement. Second, when children are engaged in activities in which they have had considerable opportunities for negotiation, their personal commitment and motivation are generally increased. Third, this is where review time is so important for teachers. If children know that regularly you and they will look at the work they have done, then they will know that their work may be evaluated by an audience of adults and peers. This process encourages children to be more self-disciplined in their attitude to completing tasks satisfactorily for their own sake, rather than for the teacher's.

What do I do next?

There are many different and ingenious mechanisms that teachers have devised for helping children move independently from one activity to the next. In the nursery environment and, I would advocate, the reception class, children will be predominantly engaged on their own self-initiated activities and there is no need for a system that moves them on. They know the resources that are available, they know how the room is organized, they know how to mix their own paints, sharpen their own pencils and get new paper or books. They are able to sustain their own momentum, moving from one experience to another as and when they are ready.

Although teachers will introduce activities to children when they are together – probably at carpet time, many children will need a reminder of what is expected of them during the day. One way that is successful with many teachers is to supply a list of some kind for children to work from. This list can be just that – a list written on the blackboard or whiteboard, it can be a piece of card in the shape of a ladder with rungs fixed by elastic or Velcro. It can be an individual 'menu', as one student called hers, tailor-made for an individual child or group. Whichever strategy is chosen, a list of some kind is an excellent way of encouraging children to be responsible for their own learning throughout the day and to give them an instant reference point of the activities on offer and to be completed.

The type of list, and what is on it, will be determined by the educational philosophy of the teacher. If children are planning their own work, choosing the order of their work and deciding with whom to work, then their work chart will be different from the class who are told what to do, when and with whom. The particular strategy that a teacher chooses will be dependent on the extent to which classroom experiences are already negotiated with children. Boxes 9.1–9.6 show some examples of ways in which teachers have introduced lists, charts and ladders to their classes. They are representative of classes at many stages of independence but all of them are reliant on the fact that a teacher has decided to give children some classroom autonomy. Many of them depend on children being given choices and making decisions and many are also dependent on the classroom having the balance of activities outlined in Chapter 4 (teacher-intensive, teacher-initiated and child-initiated activities). You may already be following a model of classroom organization and management that is similar to one of these. If you are, then there may be others that you feel ready to try out, or these examples may simply give you ideas that trigger off a composite model of your own. The exemplars may be used as points for discussion at staff meetings and in-service sessions, and my thanks go to all the innovative teachers who have shared their ideas with me and allowed me to watch them in practice. For ease of reference and

---

Box 9.1   Model 1 (from a class of 6–7-year-olds)

- The children are in fixed ability groups.
- Each group has a chart that lists the activities that the children are to do in one day.
- The activities are a mixture of teacher-initiated and teacher-intensive.
- The teacher works with different groups on the teacher-intensive tasks.
- The charts give children 'free choice' at one specific point in each day.

Issues

- The children are locked into one group, working with the same peers and work is differentiated by presumption not observation (see Chapter 6).
- The children have little independence other than moving from one activity to the next.
- The children do not have opportunities for choosing their own rhythm to their activities (see Chapter 8).
- The children have no opportunity for negotiating space and resources (see Chapter 8).
- Play is relegated to a low status activity (see Chapter 7).

---

comparison, all the exemplars have been drawn in the same format.

Reviewing

In the process of recalling what they've done, children attach language to their actions. This makes them more conscious of their actions and more able to refer to them and draw upon them for later use. Talking about, recalling and representing their actions help children evaluate and learn from their experiences. When planning and doing are followed by recall, children can build on what they've done and learned and remember it for the next time they plan an activity.

(Hohmann *et al.* 1979: 88)

Box 9.2   Model 2 (from a class of 6-year-olds)

- The children are in mixed ability groups except when they work with the teacher on teacher-intensive activities.
- Each group has its own chart.
- The children do their work in the order on the chart.
- Work on the chart is teacher-initiated, with one identified opportunity for 'choosing'.
- Work on the chart is differentiated mainly by outcome.
- The teacher draws children from these tasks to work on teacher-intensive activities that are differentiated by input.

Issues

- The children are locked into one group, working with the same peers (see Chapter 6).
- The children have little independence other than moving from one activity to the next.
- The children do not have opportunities for choosing their own rhythm to their activities (see Chapter 8).
- The children have no opportunity for negotiating space and resources (see Chapter 8).
- Play is relegated to a low status activity (see Chapter 7).

Who do children review with?

There are two main opportunities for reviewing work with children. The first of these is as the teacher has conversations with the child in the course of the working day, either when the teacher is working with children on teacher-intensive activities or when they are 'spinning the plates' of the teacher-initiated or child-initiated tasks. The second is at a time in the day when a group of children – a small group or the whole class – come together with the teacher to review what a number of children have done.

The National Literacy Strategy 'literacy hour' (DfEE 1998: 13) has drawn on this good practice in introducing a 'plenary' session. After engaging in both whole class work and group and independent work in the literacy hour, children have a plenary session with the teacher in which they 'review, reflect, consolidate

---

Box 9.3   Model 3 (from a class of 4–5-year-olds)

- The children are in 'home' (mixed ability) groups.
- Each group has its own chart.
- The chart has pictures that correspond to pictures on tables/ areas in the classroom.
- Children go to the table indicated on the chart, where activities are set out/accessible.
- Activities on the chart are teacher-initiated.
- Children can plan a child-initiated activity each time they complete one that is teacher-initiated.
- The teacher draws children out to work on teacher-intensive tasks that are usually differentiated by input.

Issues

- The children are locked into one group, working with the same peers (see Chapter 6).
- The children have limited opportunities for negotiating space and resources (because of having separate charts; see Chapter 8).
- Play is used as a 'carrot' for the completion of teacher tasks (see Chapter 7).
- The children are interrupted by the teacher when they might be engrossed in their own activity (see Chapter 9).

---

and present work'. This is a substantial move forward from the 'show-and-tell' scenario where the children did the showing and, very often, the adult did the telling. The National Literacy Strategy Framework (DfEE 1998: 13) says that 'The final plenary is at least as important as the other parts of the lesson . . . It should be used to:

- enable the teacher to spread ideas, re-emphasise teaching points, clarify misconceptions and develop new teaching points;
- enable pupils to reflect upon and explain what they have learned and to clarify their thinking;
- enable pupils to revise and practise new skills acquired in an earlier part of the lesson;

Box 9.4   Model 4 (from a class of 4–5-year-olds)

- The children are in mixed ability groups for organizational purposes only.
- There is one chart for the whole class.
- The chart shows the tables/areas where children are to work.
- The activities at these tables are teacher-initiated.
- The children can plan to do child-initiated activities whenever they choose as long as teacher-initiated tasks are completed in time.
- The work on the chart must be completed over two days.
- The teacher displays her or his own chart. This shows the teacher-intensive activities and the children with whom she or he will be working.
- The children plan the order of their work, bearing in mind whether they will be working with the teacher that day.

Issues

- Difficult to differentiate any teacher-initiated activities by input when all the children are undertaking the same activities.

- develop an atmosphere of constructive criticism and provide feedback and encouragement to pupils;
- provide opportunities for the teacher to monitor and assess the work of some pupils;
- provide opportunities for pupils to present and discuss key issues in their work.'

The National Numeracy Strategy (DfEE 1999: 15) reiterates this message; 'this part of the lesson can be used to:

- ask pupils to present and explain their work . . . so that you can question pupils about it, assess it informally and rectify any misconceptions or errors;
- discuss and compare the efficiency of pupils' different methods of calculation;
- help pupils to generalise a rule from examples generated by different groups, pairs or individuals;

Box 9.5   Model 5 (from a class of 4–5-year-olds)

- The children are in mixed ability groups for organizational purposes.
- The children begin the day choosing from the range of activities on offer while the teacher talks to parents and settles children.
- Registration happens after 30 minutes. Children do not pack activities away but know they can return to them.
- After registration the teacher and learning support assistant work with adult-intensive groups while the rest of the class engage in either teacher-initiated or child-initiated activity.
- The adults wait until the next natural break in the day (in this case, breaktime) before calling together their next adult-intensive groups.

Issues

- Some children may still be interrupted by the routines of the day (see Chapter 8) when they are already engrossed.
- Differentiation by input in teacher-initiated activities can be achieved but other children may still opt for that activity.

- draw together what has been learned, reflect on what was important about the lesson, summarise key facts, ideas and vocabulary, and what needs to be remembered;
- discuss the problems that can be solved using the ideas and skills that have been learned;
- make links to other work and discuss briefly what the class (group/individual) will go onto next;
- remind pupils about their personal targets and highlight the progress made;
- provide tasks for pupils to do at home to extend or consolidate their class work.'

Review times are invaluable as times for focusing children's attention on their work. They are also an opportunity to see who has been doing what. In both cases they provide ideal opportunities for assessment. As we shall see in the next chapter, what

---

Box 9.6   Model 6 (from a class of 5–6-year-olds)

- The children are in mixed ability groups.
- Each child has a photocopied sheet that shows the teacher-initiated activities for one week.
- Children are told at the beginning of the day if they are to work with the teacher on a teacher-intensive task.
- Children can plan child-initiated activities whenever they choose as long as teacher-initiated and teacher-intensive tasks are completed in time.
- Children mark off on their sheet when teacher-initiated tasks have been completed.
- Children record on the back of the sheet all child-initiated activities in which they have engaged.

Issues

- Difficult to differentiate any teacher-initiated activities by input if all the children are undertaking the same activities.

---

young children say by way of explanation or description about the activities in which they have engaged, reveals so much about their knowledge and understanding of the task or experience. When children review their work, the teacher (or the classroom assistant) needs a pencil and record sheet at the ready. What a child says is hard evidence of the development of their skills and concepts and is an opportunity not to be missed.

How many times a day?

If the class is operating a fairly flexible timetable, that is, one not bound by breaktimes and lunchtimes, then the optimum time to review children's work may *not* be at the end of sessions – a time when frequently there is a coming together of the class. There are good reasons for reviewing work and experiences immediately after they have concluded, but it can also be very effective if review times come at the beginning of sessions, in other words *after* playtime and after lunchtime. In this way not only does it focus children's minds back on the tasks in hand, but it can also give fresh inspiration to children as they listen to the ideas and experiences of others. This only works, of course, if children are returning to activities that were previously available and not if they are changing subject focus completely.

Wherever the review time comes I think it is most important to emphasize that it is time *after* experience that is frequently more useful to young children than time *before* it. Often teachers spend a great deal of time on elaborate introductions of new ideas and concepts about which children have very limited understanding. At this point the children have very little on which to hang these introductions and they are unable to make adequate connections with any existing knowledge. However, once they have explored, experimented with, played with new equipment, materials or ideas, they are in a much better position to come back together and talk about those experiences and their new understandings. I believe that teachers should spend less time introducing things and more time reviewing them and discussing them, once children have some experiences on which to draw.

How many children should review at once?

If in a classroom there is one teacher and 30 or more children, then it would be quite inappropriate to review what every child has done each day. This would be quite as tedious as register time and most young children would stop listening. From watching teachers experiment with this issue I would suggest that between five and six children – again depending on age – would be sufficient. If the teacher has the good fortune to be working regularly with a classroom assistant then the classroom assistant or parent can take a 'planning' group for review time. Review time should be systematic. It should ensure that children are *regularly* asked to share their experiences with others and it is recommended that teachers keep a record of the children who review at each session.

What should be reviewed?

Everything! Reviewing should include every aspect of classroom experience. This is *not* the time for only reviewing work done with or initiated by the teacher. Every aspect of work – teacher-intensive, teacher-initiated and child-initiated – should be reviewed, for all of them should have equal status in the classroom (see Chapter 4). Children are learning through every quality experience they have and the teacher needs to tap into all of these experiences in order to build a rounded profile of the child as a learner.

Conclusion

Young children are capable of an astonishing level of independence if the classroom is organized appropriately and expectations are high. Deciding on strategies for encouraging this independence is something for individual practitioners. Teachers need to be committed to any strategy they adopt (Alexander 1992) and strategies need to be introduced gradually so that children take them in their stride. When children plan, do and review their work, it gives them increased feelings of involvement in their actions and experiences. There is a far greater chance that motivation will be high and that effort will increase. As with all classroom innovation, children need to see the purpose of classroom organization and should be involved in the evaluation of its effectiveness. The final chapter examines evaluation and assessment. It is concerned with what teachers need to know about children, about classrooms and about themselves. It asserts that effective evaluation and assessment is critical if curriculum experiences are to be planned that genuinely start from the child.

10

EVALUATION AND ASSESSMENT

What teachers need to know about their children, their classrooms and themselves

Introduction

We have already established that assessment should come at the beginning of the cycle of teaching and learning, as well as at the end of it. It is rather like a sandwich in which observation is the first slice of bread, planning and doing constitute the filling, and evaluation and assessment are the final slice of bread (Fisher 1998a, 1998b, 1998c). In order to plan effectively, teachers need to know what children already know and can do and this is established through rigorous observation-based assessment of children in action and in conversation. However, there is also an important place for assessment at the end of the cycle of teaching and learning, when it is used to evaluate the effectiveness of planning and implementation.

There are three major aspects of classroom life that can be regularly evaluated in order to make changes and adjustments to increase effectiveness: children's learning, classroom organization and the quality of teaching. The three aspects are naturally interwoven, but each should be the focus of evaluation in its own right as well as part of the whole.

The evaluation of children's learning

To evaluate the quality of children's learning it is necessary to assess what children have achieved, to analyse *how* they learn as well as *what* they learn and to be conscious of their attitudes to learning. Teachers are currently involved in two kinds of assessment that serve different purposes when it comes to evaluating children's learning. *Summative assessment* presents a snapshot of the attainment of a child at one given moment and in preselected areas. *Formative assessment* is ongoing and gives teachers evidence of the developing skills and understandings of the children in their class. These two kinds of assessment have different purposes and different processes.

Summative assessment is, by definition, a summary of achievement. Very often it is required in order to pass on information about a child and therefore needs to be brief. In the course of a child's school life, summative information needs to be passed regularly to a number of different people. Parents have a legal right to receive an annual report on their child's progress, including the child's attainment in the National Curriculum, if appropriate, and feedback on baseline assessment. The next class teacher or the next school needs a summary of a child's attainment on transfer in order to help them plan the next stages of the child's education. There are long-standing discussions between teachers about how much these records should contain. Teachers writing the reports often feel that a great deal of time is spent on something that is never fully read. Teachers receiving the reports sometimes claim that they do not read them so that they can make their own unbiased judgements about each child and their attitudes and abilities. The fact remains that it is important to have a summary of each child's attainment for those times when progress is not smooth and decisions have to be made about appropriate intervention and support. Summative records of progress, written at regular intervals, can give a good indication of strengths and weaknesses, developmental patterns and gaps in knowledge and understanding, all of which can provide a foundation for the diagnostic assessment of children's current needs.

Formative records serve a different purpose. Rather than being a summary of specific points of achievement in a child's school career, formative records give ongoing information about a child's progress and attainment. Such records are necessary because they give teachers daily information about what children know and can do and therefore provide the necessary information on which to build and adjust short-term plans. As we saw in Chapter 3, short-term plans are concerned with differentiation and in order to plan activities that are appropriate for different children the teacher has to have detailed knowledge of their current learning needs. Ongoing records provide such information and are the foundation of all good planning. By dint of their concern with the detail of children's development, formative records are often quite lengthy, but these records are not for onward transmission to somebody else. The teacher uses these records either to make decisions about short-term planning or to make judgements about children's attainment for summative purposes. The records for these two forms of assessment can be summarized as follows:

Summative records are:
- brief statements made to summarize information gained through formative records;
- frequently in the form of ticklists or checklists;
- a summary of the most vital and relevant information about what the child knows, understands and can do;
- usually made at a point of transfer, for example on entry, change of class, change of school;
- designed to inform others, for example parents, next teacher/ school, outside agencies.

Formative records are:
- ongoing, cumulative records, taken throughout the teaching day;
- narrative records of what children do and what children say;
- including contributions from parents, children and other adults who work with the child;
- providing evidence on which to base future planning;
- incorporating analysis and planned action.

Recording formative assessments

Formative assessments are based on the ongoing observations that teachers make of children in action. Recording these is a demanding task, but one that teachers need to make part of their teaching day if they are to plan a curriculum that is relevant and appropriate to the children in their class. Many teachers find it helpful to have a single sheet of paper for each child on which they record the date, observation, analysis of learning and action. The *date* ensures that a child's rate of progress is recorded and that each individual spurt or plateau can be seen as part of the child's overall development. The *observation* captures what the child says and does and sets the action in context. This can be written straight on to the record sheet or it can be written on a Post-it which is then transferred to the record sheet. The *learning analysis* uses the teacher's professional judgement to identify the skills, concepts, knowledge and attitudes which the observation represents (see below). This analysis will be done at a later stage than the observation and will be used by the teacher to inform the action column. The *action* column is completed as a result of the analysis by the teacher of the learning needs of an individual child. Completion of this column prompts the teacher to fine-tune the short-term planning and ensures that assessment influences the curriculum. Sometimes no action is required above and beyond the introduction of the next planned part of the curriculum. At other times children unexpectedly reveal that they know or do not know something and the teacher needs to adjust their plans accordingly. When summative records are written they frequently draw on these detailed, ongoing notes and therefore the quality of summative records are heavily dependent on the quality of formative assessments.

Skills, concepts, knowledge and attitudes

The key to successful assessment is to be very clear about the purpose of the activity that is being assessed. When teachers plan an activity for the classroom it is usually as a result of the identification of the learning needs of an individual, a group or the class as a whole. The learning needs are expressed as skills to be learnt, concepts to be understood, knowledge to be acquired and attitudes to be adopted (see Chapter 2). These are the objectives or intentions of the activity and should drive all decisions about which activity is best planned to bring the intended learning about. When teachers begin the planning of activities with these intended learning outcomes clearly identified, then the focus of teaching is easier to sustain and the assessment of children's achievements is more easily targeted.

Assessment and the National Curriculum

It is a legal requirement in England that children are tested at the age of 7-plus and that their level of attainment is reported. This assessment is a combination of national tests administered to all 7-year-olds (previously called Standard Assessment Tasks or SATs) and Teacher Assessment (TA), which is intended to be

---

Box 10.1   Example 7: Focused teaching and assessment 1

A student had planned that a group of children should bake cakes. Her lesson plan identified the following intended learning outcomes:

1 The children will understand more fully the concept of change;
2 The children will use the scientific skills of observing, hypothesizing, predicting and investigating;
3 The children will record their findings in ways which are relevant to them in order to report back to their peers.

The lesson was well planned and the children became engrossed in their task. The student asked open-ended questions and answered the questions that the children raised. In her profiles, however, the student did not record the achievement of the children in relation to the intended learning outcomes of the lesson. Instead, she recorded the children's success in relation to the quality of the cakes that they had made. While this was important for those tasting the cakes, it was not the purpose of the lesson and the information recorded was of little value when the student came to plan the children's next scientific experience.

---

formative but which is still a summary of achievement to date. Because of its standardized format, National Curriculum testing produces data whereby one child in a class can be compared to another and a set of children in one school can be compared to a set of children in another. Since its inception there has been universal concern over the inappropriateness of subjecting children as young as 7 to any formal kind of testing (Campbell *et al.* 1993; Cox and Sanders 1994). The purpose of national testing is inherently more political than it is educational (Blenkin and Kelly 1994) for it furnishes those who want it with ammunition for proving or disproving their current manifesto on the state of the country's education system. The kind of assessment that collects summative data can be, of course, extremely attractive in terms of reducing the complexities of knowledge and understanding to a single figure or score, easily compared with others

---

Box 10.2   Example 8: Focused teaching and assessment 2

A group of 4-year-olds were to design their own Christmas wrapping paper. The purpose of the activity was for the children to use pattern in their design. The adult had brought into the class a whole range of wrapping paper as a stimulus for the children so that they could see different patterns. Following a look at this wrapping paper, it was put to one side and the child began to print their own paper. From that moment on, the support of the adult lost its focus. Rather than reminding the children about pattern and showing the purchased wrapping paper as a reminder, the adult prompted the children to use more of this colour or that shape, to fill in the spaces and to press harder to get a clearer print. In other words the adult had become more concerned with artistic rather than mathematical achievements and the potential for reinforcing a key mathematical concept (the purpose of the activity) was lost. When making assessments of that session the adult focused on the quality of the printing rather than the children's understanding and application of pattern.

---

in a column of figures. The National Curriculum tests are there, claim Gipps and Stobart (1993), to see that the curriculum is taught. They are a mechanism for checking, for overseeing the effectiveness of *teaching*. They are not concerned with the effects of learning as they do no more than summarize what a child does or does not know of the limited and subjective range of things they have been asked. Kimberley (1990) suggests that this form of assessment 'leaves no room for manoeuvre – you either achieve a target or level, or you don't'.

The work of Caroline Gipps and her colleagues strongly challenges the validity of any tests in measuring standards, let alone in raising them. However the information that standardized tests give can be useful when used alongside other, more rigorous forms of assessment. National Curriculum testing may be time-consuming, but it is not professionally rigorous. The professional demands on teachers to complete National Curriculum tests are not as great as the demands of recording formative assessments, where knowledge of young children and their development are

---

Box 10.3 Example 9: Focused teaching and assessment 3

A class of 8-year-olds were investigating an accident. It was part of their curriculum for history and their teacher had planned that they come to understand the importance of evidence in making judgements about what has happened in the past. Each group had an envelope of 'evidence' about the accident, and had to make a collaborative decision about whether the victim had had an accident or whether foul play was involved. The evidence came from the contents of the wallet of the dead man and the group had to piece together the events leading up to the accident. Throughout the discussions the teacher went from group to group listening to the children's arguments and reminding them of the task in hand. It would have been easy for the teacher to have concentrated on the discussion itself, ensuring that all took part and that the children listened to each other and so on. This she did, but first and foremost she reminded the children about the necessity for the evidence to be secure. She challenged their reasoning and asked for corroborative proof, she kept focused on the historical skills and concepts which were the purpose of the lesson. When, finally, she and the class evaluated the conclusions they had reached, the children were able to talk in terms of effective or ineffective use of evidence and because the purpose of the lesson had been so carefully sustained, assessments of the children's historical skills and understanding were easily made.

---

essential prerequisites for making sound professional analyses and judgements.

Baseline assessment

The introduction of national tests at age 7 engendered a fresh debate about what this 'proved' about a school's contribution to children's progress. The focus on attainment at ages 7, 11 and 14 meant that schools where results were high were seen to be 'good' schools and those where results were low were seen to be failing their pupils. However there are plenty of schools where children's attainment on entry is below that which might be expected nationally, where teachers do an excellent job in encouraging their children to achieve more highly than might be expected, but where they still do not reach national expectations. Conversely, there are some schools where children's attainment in tests and examinations is high, but where children are already high achievers on arrival at the school and the school has made little, or insufficient difference, to those able pupils' attainment. So began a strong campaign to establish a focus on children's progress as much as their attainment, and results started to be evaluated from benchmarks that established the starting points for children's attainment when they arrived at a school. This was relatively easy to do from Key Stage 1 to Key Stage 2 and from Key Stage 2 to Key Stage 3 and so on. However, headteachers and governors in primary, first and infant schools became concerned about how they could demonstrate the contribution they had made when there were no national assessments of children on entry to school at age 4 or 5. While many schools conducted an 'entry profile' of some kind when children were admitted, the items on the profile were frequently concerned with social skills (being independent, sharing) and fine motor skills (doing up laces, holding a pencil). While both of these areas of learning are important for young children, these entry profiles generally did not assess children in all domains and would not have provided adequate data to compare with national test results at Key Stage 1. Equally, some LEAs had established baseline assessment practices of their own and these frequently addressed reading, writing and mathematics alongside personal and social development. There was no way that such localized schemes could contribute to national data or consequently draw on national data for benchmarking and value-added comparisons. Baseline assessment practices were varied, and purposes equally so (Wolfendale 1993).

Inevitably perhaps, following extensive consultation and much debate, 1998 saw the introduction of a national framework for baseline assessment in all maintained primary schools in England (SCAA 1997). From that time, all children have been assessed within the first seven weeks of starting school (although this does not include nursery schools or classes), unless the child has been assessed at a previous school and the results have been received by the previous school, or where the assessment would not add to earlier assessment carried out in relation to a statement of special educational needs. The government did not introduce a single national baseline assessment scheme, but instead drew up accreditation criteria to be met by all potential scheme providers and schools have been able to choose from some 91 different baseline assessment schemes that met the accreditation criteria of the Qualifications and Curriculum Authority (QCA, the successors of SCAA).

The first children to be assessed using an accredited baseline assessment scheme took their national tests at age 7 in 2000 and this has given some schools their first opportunity to demonstrate progress from entry to age 7. However, the only reliable data is from those schemes that incorporate the QCA Baseline Assessment Scales (QCA 1997) as part of their scheme. Only these schemes have national data that can be used in analysis of children's progress. Regrettably even the robustness of this data is open to serious question. There are substantial concerns about the reliability of assessments that are conducted by a range of teachers in a range of ways at different times in a child's school experience – the difference between week one and week seven of a young children's schooling is highly significant. Reliability as a characteristic of assessment is 'concerned with the accuracy with which the test measures the skill or attainment it is designed to measure' (Gipps 1994: 67). The basic question underlying issues of reliability is: would an assessment produce the same or a similar score on two occasions or if given by two assessors? The accreditation criteria for baseline assessment schemes (SCAA 1997: 7) requires that scheme providers demonstrate 'planned procedures for ensuring the quality and consistency of assessments carried out as part of its scheme'. Nevertheless, the fact that there are some 91 different schemes nationally makes comparison impossible and moderation, other than within schools or between schools using the same scheme, largely a waste of time.

While the principles of establishing a national framework for baseline assessment are understood (if not accepted) by most practitioners, its introduction has thrown up a number of significant problems. The first is that children are different ages on admission to school. Some children are just 4 and some are over 5 years old. This means that data must be interpreted carefully if comparisons with neighbouring schools or authorities are not to be misinterpreted. It can also bring problems if the results from older children are interpreted as these children being 'brighter'.

Then comparison with results at the end of Key Stage 1 becomes invidious because it appears that the children have made insufficient progress, whereas in fact they have simply had less time to make progress (having gone into school later, but taken their national tests at age 7 at the same time as all other children in all other authorities). A second problem has been the significant difference in children's achievement between their first week in school and their seventh. If schools try and demonstrate the greatest extent of their value-added contribution then they will want to assess children as early as possible after admission. There are opportunities for conflict here between nursery and reception/Year 1 assessments. Nursery teachers, who have often known children for three to five terms of their development, will have made assessments of what they know and can do on transfer to school. Nursery teachers usually want to be positive and demonstrate what children *can* do. Baseline assessment identifies what children *cannot* do, and consequently assessments between these two phases of education – which should dovetail very smoothly – are sometimes very disjointed. It is often difficult for some reception/Year 1 teachers to draw on and build on the assessments made by their preschool colleagues. Where a school has a nursery on site this is a relatively straightforward process, but where a school receives children from six, eight or ten preschool settings then continuity and progression is far more difficult to achieve. One serious complaint about the existing baseline assessment framework is that the staff who know most about the children (that is, nursery and preschool staff) do not undertake the baseline assessment and those teachers who should be spending time getting to know their children, and their parents and carers (that is, reception and Year 1 staff), are asked to make important assessments based on little previous knowledge and experience. This is not appropriate for children within their first few weeks at school. At a time when children need to be most secure and receive most attention from reception and Year 1 teachers, staff are diverted to complete this external assessment and sometimes find themselves resorting to inappropriate practices to achieve it. The final concern is that one assessment tool is purporting to achieve two assessment purposes. The two key purposes of baseline assessment are:

- to provide information to help teachers plan effectively to meet children's individual learning needs; and

- to measure children's attainment, using one or more numerical outcomes which can be used in later value-added analyses of children's progress.

To begin with, the two purposes of baseline assessment are quite different in terms of assessment procedure (Fisher 1998d). One is essentially short-term and the other, by definition, long-term. While one needs to be ongoing, the other has to be a one-off snapshot in time. In other words, one is formative, the other summative. As we have seen, both these processes are present in good assessment procedures, but the question is, can one assessment tool be used to meet both purposes? First, the ongoing observations and conversations of formative assessment cover all aspects of the curriculum. If assessment is to be used to support teacher planning then it cannot be selective. Second, good formative assessment does not interrupt normal classroom practice. Children are assessed in contexts in which they are secure and confident and the teacher is able to make assessments over different periods of time, at different times of the day and in a range of learning situations. Third, formative assessment gathers evidence of children in a range of social contexts: both with and without the teacher or another adult, both with or without other children. It also involves observation of activities that have been initiated by teachers and those which children have initiated for themselves. Finally, formative assessment frequently involves the judgements of more than one adult. Over time, the assessments and records of a number of adults involved in and concerned with the education of a child build into a comprehensive profile of that child as a learner. The judgements of the nursery nurse, the classroom assistant, the educational psychologist, the specialist teacher, the parent and the child himself or herself combine to give a substantial body of information and evidence of the achievements of each child from which their current abilities can be summarized and their future learning needs identified.

The *National Framework for Baseline Assessment* (SCAA 1997) requires any accredited scheme to include both formative and summative processes. It makes reference to the formative dimension when it says that schemes must 'include clear guidance to teachers on how the outcomes of the assessment can be used to inform the planning both for a class and for individual children' (1997: 6). The *Framework* then highlights the summative dimension when it requires schemes to 'provide one or two numerical outcomes capable of being used or later value-added analysis'. Having alluded to both purposes in its guidance, however, there is a requirement only to carry out and report on one dimension, and that is the one that will produce the numerical outcomes for value-added purposes. The message is that it may be *desirable* to carry out the formative element of the process, but only *necessary* to carry out the summative exercise.

I have suggested that in order to be effective in informing future planning, formative assessment needs to:

- assess all the curriculum in order to support the planning of the whole curriculum;
- be part of the normal work of the classroom, not something added or extra;
- take place over time/in a range of contexts/with and without support/during child-initiated and adult-initiated activities;
- involve a range of people, including other professionals, parents and the child.

The summative dimension of the *National Framework for Baseline Assessment* (SCAA 1997: 6) only requires schemes to assess three areas of learning, and not even all aspects of these. Schemes must cover 'aspects of language and literacy, mathematics and personal and social development'. There is no compulsory assessment of children's creative or physical development, or their knowledge and understanding of the world, and many aspects of literacy, language and mathematics are missing. How can this assessment be used to help teachers plan effectively to meet every aspect of children's learning needs if more than three-quarters of the curriculum is not assessed?

Second, the *Framework* (1997: 9) gives guidance that 'many of the assessments included in a baseline assessment scheme will take place during normal classroom activities' and that assessments will focus on what 'children are typically able to do, in normal classroom conditions'. However, if a teacher has only known a child a matter of days, and those days are the first of the child's experience of school, it is difficult to imagine how 'typical' this can be. From the child's point of view it is highly unlikely that in the first seven weeks of school, classroom conditions will be 'normal'. For many children this may be their first time away from home, they may be adjusting to new surroundings, new people, new expectations and new emotions – hardly a 'normal'

situation for anybody, let alone a young child, and hardly the
ideal circumstances in which to be making judgements about
that child's ability.

While both SCAA and QCA documentation is explicit in its
guidance that baseline assessments should be part of the everyday process of teaching and learning, there are counter-messages
that have subverted this good intention. The Guidance (SCAA
1997: 9) says that

> If . . . a scheme requires teachers to assess or record these
> assessments in such a way that teachers cannot teach the
> rest of the class in the normal way, the maximum time for
> this should not normally exceed 20 minutes per child, on
> average, or two days for a class of thirty children.

The very suggestion that there is a time limit to baseline assessment suggests that it is something extra, something more than
usual classroom practice and that this something extra will be
time-consuming. This has been one of the least helpful elements
of SCAA/QCA's advice for, while it is important to protect teachers from unreasonable demands on their valuable time, it is not
helpful to suggest that this will result from the assessments themselves. Assessment should be an integral part of the teacher's role
and not an added extra. If time is to be allocated it should be for
the completion of the administration, not the completion of the
assessments.

Third, there is an issue of time for teachers to do assessments
in a range of contexts, where children are working with and
without support and during teacher-initiated and child-initiated
activities. Within the requirements of the National Framework,
time is precisely what teachers do not have. In order to make the
necessary judgements in a very limited amount of time, teachers
are likely to give children prescriptive and directed tasks just in
order to feel secure that the baseline assessment scales have been
covered.

Finally, the *National Framework for Baseline Assessment* (SCAA
1997) does not require the involvement of any person other than
the teacher. It can be completed without any reference to parents, carers or other practitioners and as such may suffer from
bias and possible lack of depth. The adage that two – or more –
heads are better than one can justifiably be applied to the assessment scenario. Using the current *Framework*, it is simply not

possible for national baseline assessment to meet both its intended purposes.

Within the current baseline assessment model, there are also a number of conflicts of interest. The *reception teacher* (and Year 1 teacher) is expected to make judgements 'over time' but 'within seven weeks'. Those assessments may be made at the expense of time spent settling children and parents into a new class. There may be no preschool records to draw on and such records as the school does receive may be of variable content and quality. There is also the conflict that stems from the use of the assessments for value-added purposes. When a school wants to demonstrate the progress a child has made, it is not always in the school's interests to have the child achieve highly on baseline assessment.

The *nursery teacher* on the other hand, has the conflict of wanting and being able to demonstrate what progress the child has made since being in the nursery, while knowing that this contribution will not be counted for value-added purposes. Nursery teachers will have made assessments of children in a range of contexts over maybe three or five terms and yet not be asked to make the summative assessments that they are so well placed to make.

For *parents* there may be conflict surrounding the purposes of baseline assessment. The reported incidents of parents going to schools and asking how they can prepare their children for the baseline assessment tests shows a misunderstanding about baseline and its purposes. If the child has attended a preschool or nursery there may be a conflict between the assessments made in that setting – demonstrating achievement, and starting from what the child *can* do, and those made in the reception class, which must report on what the child *cannot* do. There may be conflict too, for parents, about their role in the assessment process. While schools and the government talk about partnership with parents, and of parents being their child's first and enduring educators, this is not confirmed by the *Framework*'s single requirement that teachers should 'explain the outcomes of assessment to parents' (SCAA 1997: 6).

For *children* there is potential conflict surrounding the whole baseline assessment process. At a time when they may be vulnerable and unsettled they are expected to perform well and show what they know and can do. At a time when they most want adult time and attention their teacher may be required to be with someone else in order to complete their assessments. At a time when they most want to do what is familiar and comforting they may be exposed to practices that are confusing and threatening. Of course the *Framework* does not require any of this, but the reality of classroom practice amidst the welter of other pressures on reception class teachers means that all of these conflicts can arise.

Warwick University (Lindsay *et al.* 2000: 5) has completed an evaluation of all the accredited baseline assessment schemes and has concluded, amongst other things, that:

- teachers see a tension between pedagogic purposes (e.g. assessment for teaching, identification of special educational needs or SEN) and assessment for 'value-added';
- schools are required to offer parents the opportunity to discuss the outcomes of baseline assessment, but this has not been developed effectively in many schools;
- headteachers in particular would like a move to a single national baseline assessment scheme, particularly to show the effectiveness of their own school;
- for 'value-added' and the measurement of progress for other purposes (e.g. threshold payments) it is necessary to be sure each accredited scheme is rigorous in terms of the reliability and validity of scores, and that there is comparability between schemes.

In October 2000 the QCA announced a new consultation on national baseline assessment and its primary purpose will be to determine the desirability of moving to a single national baseline assessment for value-added purposes and to consider moving the timing of baseline assessment to the end of the Foundation Stage, that is, the end of the reception year.

Assessment in the early years

National Curriculum summative assessment practices are in stark contrast to strategies used in early years settings to build a rounded profile of the child as a learner. Mary Jane Drummond (1993) effectively summarizes early years assessment practices as *seeing* children's learning, *understanding* it and then *putting* our understanding to good use. It is important to examine the key elements of assessment in the early years in order to ensure that practice is once again rooted in principle. The headings that I have used draw on the excellent chapter by Vicky Hurst and

Margaret Lally (1992) in a book devoted to the subject of assessment in early childhood education (Blenkin and Kelly 1992).

1 *It is rooted in developmentally appropriate practice.* Children are active learners (EYCG 1992) engaged in building their own cognitive jigsaw of experiences. If teachers are to understand what personal models are being constructed then the assessment they use must be open to evidence of learning from the perspective of the child. Children bring to school their own conceptions and misconceptions (Gilbert and Osborne 1982; Harlen 1985) and these are sometimes far more difficult to change than teachers might imagine (Postlethwaite 1993). However, if teachers are committed to closely observing what children do and say as the foundations of their assessment practices, then they will have valuable and accurate information on which to base future activities and experiences.

2 *It occurs in contexts with which children are familiar.* Marion Whitehead (1992) reminds us that there is a considerable body of knowledge that shows that young children's demonstrated knowledge is radically affected by the social and physical constraints of their immediate surroundings (see also Heath 1983; Tizard and Hughes 1984; Wells 1985; Barrett 1989). If children are assessed in unfamiliar contexts, contexts in which they feel inhibited or insecure, then the results of that assessment will not be a true reflection of what the child knows and can do. If children are set unfamiliar tasks that do not enable them to draw on previous *successful* experiences then they are unlikely to do themselves justice.

3 *It is based on what children can do rather than what they cannot.* Tina Bruce's (1987) famous principle of early childhood education has been used and developed in a whole range of documents about early years practice. It is such an important principle because it gives the process of assessment a particularly positive tone. Rather than adopting the deficit model of testing, which seeks to determine what a child *cannot* do, it starts from what the child can do, or can nearly do (Roberts 1995b). The onus, then, is on the teacher to match the curriculum to the child and not to try and fit the child into the curriculum.

4 *It acknowledges that learning is not compartmentalized under subject headings.* National Curriculum assessment is divided into subjects and different status is awarded to the subjects within

---

Box 10.4   Example 10: The cross-curricular nature of learning

When engaged in a cooking activity the children may gain experience of English (when discussing the processes involved or consulting the recipe), maths (when counting out spoonfuls, comparing sizes, weights etc.), science (when observing changes or dissolving substances), design and technology (when observing the effects certain tools such as a whisk have on the ingredients), history (when discussing how cake mixture was beaten before we had whisks), geography (when discussing which part of the world certain recipes come from and finding these on a map), personal and social development (when learning about the hygiene aspects of food preparation, and about which foods are most and least healthy), music (when comparing or imitating vocally sounds made by different utensils), physical education (when learning to control whisks, knives, cutters etc.) and art (when discussing patterns made by different implements, or decorating cakes or biscuits).

(Hurst and Lally 1992: 55)

---

it (Whitehead's 1992 'first' and 'second' division subjects). However, observation of young children engaged in developmentally appropriate practice shows how well planned activities and experiences cut across all boundaries and enable children to draw on a range of cross-curricular knowledge and understanding. Hurst and Lally give a good example in Box 10.4.

5 *It recognizes that young children learn best from activities that they are motivated to choose for themselves.* Note the terminology 'motivated to choose'. Sometimes teachers plan the teaching day as though children are only motivated to do what they have selected for themselves, and that usually involves playing. So children have to do what the teacher has initiated before being allowed to 'choose' what they want to do. My experience in classrooms shows quite unequivocally that skilful teachers initiate such interesting activities and experiences that children are often every bit as absorbed and involved in them as those they initiate for themselves. Children can and should be motivated by the planned curriculum, but this is

more likely to happen when they also have ongoing opportunities to engage in activities that they have initiated for themselves. If the activities that children prefer are always those they have initiated for themselves then perhaps the teacher needs to reflect on her or his own planning. Assessment needs to be of activities that teachers have initiated and that children have initiated for themselves. In settings where these are motivating, children demonstrate knowledge, skills and understandings that may not be evident in less motivating contexts (Donaldson 1978; Hughes 1986).

6 *It stresses that children's learning and achievements are affected by the relationships they have formed with their peers and with adults.* Children, like adults, achieve most in an atmosphere that gives them confidence and enhances their self-esteem (Dowling 1995, 2000; Roberts 1995a). The relationships that form the bedrock of classrooms are best developed in an atmosphere of mutual respect and trust. Classrooms in which children have opportunities to be independent and to negotiate their learning experiences build up that respect and trust between pupils and between children and their teachers.

7 *It is informed by all those who know about and are interested in the development of the child.* A rounded profile is jointly created by people who see the child in different contexts and in different ways. Parents are their children's first educators and their continuing knowledge of their own child gives valuable insights into their individual needs and interests. Other adults who work with the child – such as child-minders, playgroup leaders, speech therapists, health visitors and educational psychologists – all have and make their specialist contributions which should be valued and used.

8 *It is rooted in principles of equality of opportunity and the celebration of diversity.* Many of the materials used in tests are 'culturally alien' to many bilingual and working-class children (Gipps and Stobart 1993). The revised National Curriculum still does not identify a place for the languages of many bilingual British-born children. Whitehead (1992: 103) suggests that 'by actually naming "English" as a core language component for all schools we lose a crucial perspective on the central role of any human language in cognition and personal and cultural development'. Early years assessment practices recognize individuality and, therefore, diversity. The planning of an appropriate curriculum draws on the current and previous experiences of children,

and inevitably includes the distinctive features of their culture and communities. It is crucial that practitioners constantly scrutinize the context and content of their planned activities to ensure that materials are not culturally biased, and that they do not portray stereotypical images or militate against the everyday experience or interest of girls as opposed to boys.

Making value judgements

Educational assessment is an imprecise activity (Blenkin and Kelly 1992) in that it must depend to a great extent on judgements and those judgements can never be neutral. We bring to any assessment of children all our own expectations, presumptions, preferences and bias. Of course, just because we cannot make truly neutral judgements does not mean that we abandon the practice altogether, rather we must become more aware of our own value systems and what we as assessors are likely to bring to any assessment situation. Drummond *et al.* in their training materials *Making Assessment Work* (1992) warn that it is all too easy to make judgements based on assumptions about what we *expect* children to do, to think, to feel and to be and not on what children *actually* do.

Making time for assessment

Chapter 2 explained why observation and conversation are the key strategies on which early years assessments should be based. Both of these require teachers' close attention and it can be difficult in a large class to find the time for either, unless the children are encouraged to be independent learners. Chapter 4 suggested ways in which teachers can make time for assessment but these are all based on the maxim that time must be planned. Assessment is too important to be fitted in when there is a spare moment or attempted when children are demanding attention. While some assessment clearly takes place when an adult is working with a group, this is not sufficient. Some observations require the adult to be independent of children, and this requires children to be able to work independently of adults.

Planning the use of time for assessment

The following is a useful checklist for planning the use of time for formative assessment:

- What evidence is required?
- Is the assessment to find out what children *already* know/can do or what they know/can do *after* a period of teaching?
- Is the evidence best gathered during or after the activity?
- Who will gather the evidence?
- What technique best serves the assessment purpose?
- How and by whom will the evidence be recorded?

Gathering evidence of children's learning

What evidence is required?

There is a difference between obtaining *information* about children's learning and gathering *evidence* of their learning. We collect *information* about children's learning:

- from previous summative records;
- from parent consultations;
- from conversations with the child.

All of these are important but are not sufficient. Information can be dated or open to misinterpretation. Effective planning is based on current *evidence* and is gathered in a variety of ways:

- through the collection of tangible end-products;
- through photocopying pictures/writing/mark-making etc.;
- through taking photographs;
- through making audio/video recordings;
- through observation of what children do:
  - the process of learning,
  - their learning styles and strategies,
  - their knowledge and understanding,
  - their skills and attitudes;
- through recording what children say:
  - their developing understandings,
  - their misunderstandings,
  - their explanations,
  - their enthusiasms.

Is the assessment to find out what children already know/ can do or what they know/can do after a period of teaching?

Both these kinds of evidence are important. It is perfectly legitimate to make assessments of the effectiveness of our own teaching.

However, there is another and equally important kind of evidence that teachers require in order to have a starting point for children's future learning. Chapter 4 describes those open-ended activities that give teachers knowledge about what children bring to a learning experience. This is the kind of evidence teachers need before planning rather than after teaching and, bearing in mind these two purposes, teachers need to make professional decisions about the appropriate timing of assessments.

Is the evidence best gathered during or after the activity?

When there is the opportunity, observation-based assessment gives teachers their best first-hand evidence. There are, however, occasions when observation is neither feasible nor sufficient. When there is only one teacher in a classroom – or even when there are more adults – it is simply not possible to make observations of the learning of more than one individual or small group of children at any one time. Therefore there are times when teachers need to talk with children after an activity is finished in order to find out what they did and what they now understand. Sometimes teachers want to give children the opportunity to describe their experiences either to an adult and/or to their peers (see the section on reviewing in Chapter 9). In this instance, conversations become the key strategy.

Who will gather the evidence, where and when?

- Who? (adults)
  - the teacher,
  - another adult;

- With whom? (the children)
  - child alone,
  - children together,
  - children working with the teacher,
  - children working with another adult,
  - children working without an adult;

- Where?
  - inside the classroom,
  - outside the classroom,
  - in the hall,
  - in the playground;

- When?
  - before or after teaching,
  - while working with child/children,
  - while child/children working independently.

What technique best serves the assessment purpose?

There are a variety of assessment techniques which all have their value. The decision that teachers have to make is which technique will give them the evidence they need. For excellent descriptions of different techniques and their uses, for example time sampling, frequency sampling, audiotaping and targeted observation, see Drummond *et al.* (1992) and Bartholomew and Bruce (1993).

How and by whom will the evidence be recorded?

Certain kinds of evidence 'speaks for itself'. Pieces of writing, photographs, tape recordings and photocopies only need annotation to make them valuable evidence of the stage in a child's development. The annotation is important, however, for without it the precise context for learning will be forgotten. Evidence of this kind should be annotated with:

- the name of the child;
- the date;
- the learning context;
- child's comments (if any);
- level of support from adult(s)/other children (if any);
- Foundation Stage Stepping Stone level statement (if appropriate);
- National Curriculum level description (if appropriate).

When evidence is of what children do or say, then it is up to adults to record this in a way that is both efficient and effective. The learning materials on assessment prepared by Mary Jane Drummond and her colleagues (1992) give helpful exemplars of methods of writing down observations and assessments.

Self-assessment

An important element in children's involvement in their own learning is the opportunity they have for self-assessment. When children are engaged in making decisions about what they have done and how they have done it, then it inevitably adds to their self-esteem. If children only ever receive judgements about their work and their achievements from adults, then they will not learn the critical life skill of self-motivation. Here are some questions that teachers believe encourage children to reflect on themselves as learners:

- What interests me?
- What do I enjoy doing?
- What do I want to be able to do?
- What helps me to learn?
- What would I like to know?

These questions can support a child in reviewing a particular piece of work, an activity or an experience:

- Do I know what I want to achieve?
- Do I think I need help?
- Do I know who/how to go about getting help?
- Have I thought how this might be evaluated?
- How will I evaluate it?

In Chapter 8 we saw how children can be involved in determining the criteria for success in an activity. Children have their own and very clear perceptions of classroom and school experiences. It might be an interesting exercise to imagine what the children in your class might answer if they were asked the above questions . . . then ask them, and see if you were right!

Evaluating classroom organization

Teachers carry out other observations in classrooms that are not specifically to do with the development of individual children. These are concerned with how smoothly the class runs, how cooperative children are, whether good use is being made of space and resources and whether the classroom environment is contributing to the quality of children's learning. This information can be gathered in different ways, and here I have identified four possibilities.

Observation of one child

This observation provides evidence of the organization and planning of experiences:

- Does the child move purposefully from one activity to the next?
- Are there times when the child wastes time, by queuing for example?
- Does the child know how to be independent, or does he or she frequently turn to other children or adults for support?
- Are the child's experiences positive?
- Are the child's experiences balanced and appropriate?

Observation of one activity

This observation provides evidence of the responses of different children to the same planned activity:

- How do children's responses to the activity differ?
- Is the activity successful in meeting the needs of all the children for whom it was planned?
- Are children learning what was intended?
- If not, does their learning lead the teacher to new understandings about the nature of the activity or the interests of the children?

Observation of the whole class

This observation is planned to highlight issues of space, resourcing, interaction and independence:

- Is there sufficient space in the classroom for children to engage in active learning?
- Are all the tables and areas in the classroom used effectively, or are some wasting space?
- Are resources easily accessible for children?
- Do children responsibly return resources to their appropriate location?
- Do children interrupt their peers and adults unnecessarily?
- Are children able to manage themselves independently?

Observation of the teacher

This is perhaps the most challenging but potentially the most enlightening observation of all:

- What do I spend my time doing in the classroom?
- Do I spend more time talking than the children?
- Do I listen to children as well as initiate conversations?

- Do I ask children questions to which I already know the answers?
- Have I planned activities that interest and engage the children?
- Am I interrupted unnecessarily by children?
- What strategies am I using to make children more independent?
- At the end of the day have I done what I planned to do?

In order to support teachers in carrying out an audit of their current provision and practice, the Oxfordshire Early Years Development and Childcare Partnership have designed a quality framework for the Foundation Stage, which suggests key indicators of quality provision and practice (see Box 10.5). All of these indicators were taken from reports on early years education: the HMI report, *The Education of Children Under Five* (DES 1989); the Rumbold Report, *Starting with Quality* (DES 1990); the report of the National Commission on Education, *Learning to Succeed* (1993) and the report of the RSA *Start Right: The Importance of Early Learning* (Ball 1994). The consensus within these documents about what constitutes high quality provision and practice in the early years is overwhelming. It might be useful to share this audit with those who are responsible for and manage schools, to ensure that children in the early years are receiving their entitlement.

The quality of teaching

Reflective practice

> The importance of self-knowledge for the educator is plainly spelled out: effective educators are those whose work includes the study of themselves, their knowledge, their feelings and the frameworks within which they understand children.
>
> (Drummond 1993: 117)

Teachers sometimes spend so long monitoring and assessing the performance of children that they forget that the process is as important for themselves. Yet it is as crucial that teachers assess themselves as it is that they assess their class. Being a professional educator requires teachers to be continually developing their own practice and this is not possible unless time is set aside to be reflective and open to change.

The notion of reflective teaching stems from John Dewey (1933) who contrasted 'routine action' with 'reflective action'. According to Dewey, routine action is guided by factors such as tradition and

Box 10.5   Oxfordshire Quality Framework for the Foundation Stage

PROVISION

(a) Available space is maximized for play and active learning

indoors
- is the most appropriate space allocated to 3-, 4- and 5-year-old learners (e.g. size, flooring, sinks)?
- is there sufficient space for play and active learning? (e.g. are tables and chairs kept to a minimum?)
- is there easy access to an outside area for play and active learning?
- are areas for play constantly available?

outdoors
- is there an outdoor area for play and active learning?
- is the area safe and easily accessible?
- is this area securely fenced off?
- is equipment appropriate for the age of children?

(b) A rich variety of resources are provided for outdoor and indoor experiences

- is money allocated to play resources as part of the setting's Development Plan?
- are there sufficient play resources of good quality in the setting?
- is there a range of appropriate, good quality resources outside, e.g. wheeled toys, small PE equipment (balls, hoops, bean-bags), sand, construction, climbing apparatus?
- are resources well organized and accessible to children?

(c) Appropriate facilities for the age of children

- are there sufficient toilets for the number of children (minimum of 1 toilet to 10 children)?
- is there easy access to these toilets?
- is there a private area for children who have 'accidents'?
- is there sufficient furniture of suitable size and height?

- is there access to a sink in the setting of the appropriate height?

(d) An appropriate ratio of adults to children – all the time

- is there a ratio of:
  - 1:13 in LEA nursery classes/Early Years Units?
  - 1:10 in LEA nursery schools; voluntary and private settings with a qualified teacher and NNEB (or equivalent)?
  - 1:8 in voluntary or private settings with staff who have other appropriate early years qualifications?
- is the quality of support adequate?
  - is it available for the whole session?
  - is it provided by the same person?

(e) Appropriately trained and experienced educators with a knowledge of child development

- is the educator trained to teach 3-, 4- and 5-year-olds?
- has the educator undertaken further training in early childhood education?
- has staff appropriate qualification/training for working with 3-, 4- and 5-year-olds?

PRACTICE

(f) Strong home/setting partnerships

- are parents given helpful information about the educational provision?
- is there an appropriate induction programme for children and parents?
- are parents encouraged to contribute to assessments by sharing observations of their child's learning at home?
- are parents well informed about their child's progress and achievements?
- do parents have good opportunities to be involved with their child's learning?
- are personal contexts of children's families, cultures and communities valued?
- is the setting's work enriched by links with the community?

(g) Quality of teaching

- do educators have a secure knowledge and understanding of all the areas of learning?
- do educators have appropriately high expectations of children?
- do educators employ an appropriate range of teaching strategies?
- are methods and organization 'fit for purpose'?
- is exposition and explanation informative, lively, well-structured and well-paced?
- does the use of questions probe children's knowledge and understanding and challenge their thinking?
- do educators join in, support and extend play where appropriate?
- do educators make good use of available time, space and resources?
- do educators manage children well and achieve appropriate standards of behaviour?

(h) Planning which meets the needs and interests of 3-, 4- and 5-year-olds

- is the planned curriculum based on the Early Learning Goals?
- is the curriculum planned with full regard to children's gender, race, ability and spirituality?
- are written policies in place which fulfil statutory requirements?
- are there effective written plans for all areas of learning, demonstrating breadth and balance?
- does planning support steady progression and offer continuity of learning?
- does planning address the different needs and abilities of children, including those with SEN?
- does planning recognize the importance of learning which is initiated by children, as well as that which is initiated by adults?
- is short-term planning sufficiently flexible to be informed by observation-based assessment?

- does planning identify intended learning in terms of concepts, skills, knowledge and attitudes?
- do staff regularly evaluate the outcomes of their planning?

(i) Assessment of children's attainment and progress

- do staff assess children's attainment and progress in all areas of learning?
- are assessments based on observation of and conversations with children?
- are assessment made of both adult initiated and child initiated learning (including play)?
- are children helped to assess their own achievements?
- are parent contributions incorporated in the assessment process?
- do staff keep manageable records both for themselves and for others?
- do staff complete formative and summative records in line with the Oxfordshire Baseline Assessment Scheme?
- do assessments provide the basis for future planning?
- is each child's attainment a reflection of their ability?

(j) An appropriate curriculum, both indoors and outdoors

- is the full curriculum (through planning and practice) represented both indoors and outdoors?
- does the curriculum meet the needs and interests of individual children?
- do children have sustained opportunities for learning, without unnecessary interruptions?

(k) Attitudes, interactions and personal development

- do children make constructive relationships with one another and with adults?
- are children confident, do they show appropriate self-esteem and are they given respect?
- are children able to concentrate and persevere on both child-initiated and adult-initiated learning?
- do children show initiative and are they given responsibility?

habit and by institutional definitions and expectations. Reflect-ive action on the other hand involves a willingness to engage in constant self-appraisal and development. It requires teachers to be flexible and to be willing to analyse rigorously their current practice in order to bring about change. Pollard and Tann (1993: 9) identify six key characteristics of reflective practice:

1 Reflective teaching implies an active concern with aims and consequences, as well as means and technical efficiency.
2 Reflective teaching is applied in a cyclical or spiralling process, in which teachers monitor, evaluate and revise their own prac-tice continuously.
3 Reflective teaching requires competence in methods of classroom enquiry, to support the development of teaching competence.
4 Reflective teaching requires attitudes of open-mindedness, re-sponsibility and wholeheartedness.
5 Reflective teaching is based on teacher judgement, which is informed partly by self-reflection and partly by insights from educational disciplines.
6 Reflective teaching, professional learning and personal fulfil-ment are enhanced through collaboration and dialogue with colleagues.

Action research

One rigorous way in which many teachers now adopt the pro-cess of reflection is through engaging in action research in their own settings. Action research has two essential aims – to *improve* and to *involve*. The involvement is critical to the practitioner. Instead of research that makes judgements on the teacher, it is the teacher who is in a position to control what is to be studied and how. Teachers also determine what should be done with any outcomes – are they for their own reflective purposes or could they be used for further study or for sharing with a wider body of colleagues and professionals?

Carr and Kemmis (1986) claim that action research provides a means of 'becoming critical' and they identified a cyclic model of planning, acting, observing and reflecting which encapsulated Schön's (1987) notion of 'reflection-on-action'. Handal's sug-gestion (quoted in Day 1993), is that the normal conditions for school based action research may well be such that an incomplete 'self-reflective' cycle occurs and teachers spend most of their time planning and acting and less time observing and reflecting. There has always been a tendency for this to happen in schools but we have seen that it is reflection and action that are the key ways in which teachers improve their practice.

An examination of practice in systematic ways can, of course, challenge existing theories and beliefs. In action research, say Pollard and Tann (1993), practitioners must be prepared to explore the discrepancies between their current practice and the new insights that might be acquired. Whatever methodology is used by teachers, the notion of self-evaluation is every bit as critical for them as it is for children. Reflection should lead to new ways of working (Adelman 1985) and in order for this to happen teachers need to be explorers and enquirers in the best traditions of early years practice.

Conclusion

Evaluation and assessment practices are crucial because they can bring about change. Research and experience are constantly informing the dynamic nature of classroom pedagogy and the outcomes of reflection on practice lead teachers to make improvements for both children and themselves. The quality of children's experiences at school are a result of the effectiveness of teachers in evaluating their own performance, as well as the performance of children, and having the knowledge and skills to translate their evaluations into effective planning and teaching.

Assessment lays the foundations for quality teaching and learning. When teachers watch and listen to children they put themselves in the role of learner alongside their pupils, finding out what they know and can do. Observation of children in action reveals just what a range of competences young learners have acquired. It reveals how differently young children approach their learning and what a range of needs and interests they have. When teachers get to know children this well it becomes impossible to fit them all into the same curriculum mould. The competences of young learners demand that teachers respond to children's individual and idiosyncratic learning needs. If the planned curriculum is to be relevant and purposeful then what is taught and learnt in classrooms needs to start from the individual learner – it needs to start from the child.

REFERENCES

Adelman, C. (1985) Action research, in S. Hegarty and P. Evans (eds) *Research Methods in Special Education*. Windsor: NFER.

Adelman, C. (1992) Play as a quest for vocation, *Journal of Curriculum Studies*, 24 (2): 139–51.

Alexander, R. (1992) *Policy and Practice in Primary Education*. London: Routledge.

Alexander, R., Rose, J. and Whitehead, C. (1992) *Classroom Organisation and Classroom Practice in Primary Schools: A Discussion Paper*. London: DES.

Anning, A. (1991) *The First Years at School*. Buckingham: Open University Press.

Athey, C. (1990) *Extending Thought in Young Children: A Parent–Teacher Partnership*. London: Paul Chapman.

Aubrey, C. (ed.) (1994) *The Role of Subject Knowledge in the Early Years of Schooling*. London: Falmer Press.

Ball, C. (1994) *Start Right: The Importance of Early Learning*. London: RSA.

Barnes, D., Britton, J. and Rosen, H. (1969) *Language, the Learner and the School*. Harmondsworth: Penguin.

Barnes, D. and Todd, F. (1977) *Communication and Learning in Small Groups*. London: Routledge and Kegan Paul.

Barrett, G. (ed.) (1989) *Disaffection From School? The Early Years*. Lewes: Falmer Press.

Bartholomew, L. and Bruce, T. (1993) *Getting to Know You*. London: Hodder and Stoughton.

Bealing, D. (1972) Organisation of junior school classrooms, *Educational Research*, 14: 231–5.

Bennett, N., Desforges, C., Cockburn, A. and Wilkinson, B. (1984) *The Quality of Pupil Learning Experiences*. Hove: Lawrence Erlbaum.

Bennett, N. and Kell, J. (1989) *A Good Start? Four Year Olds in Infant Schools*. Oxford: Basil Blackwell.

Bennett, N., Wood, L. and Rogers, S. (1997) *Teaching Through Play: Teachers' Thinking and Classroom Practice*. Buckingham: Open University Press.

Bilton, H. (1994) Morning and afternoon sessions in the nursery, do they have equal status? With particular reference to story time, *International Journal of Early Years Education*, 2 (2): 54–64.

Blenkin, G.M. and Kelly, A.V. (eds) (1987) *Early Childhood Education: A Developmental Curriculum*. London: Paul Chapman.

Blenkin, G.M. and Kelly, A.V. (eds) (1992) *Assessment in Early Childhood Education*. London: Paul Chapman.

Blenkin, G.M. and Kelly, A.V. (eds) (1994) *The National Curriculum and Early Learning*. London: Paul Chapman.

Brierley, J. (1994) *Give Me a Child Until He is Seven*, 2nd edn. London: Falmer Press.

Britton, J. (1970) Speech in the school, *NATE Journal*, summer 1970: 22–4.

Bronson, M.B. (2000) *Self-Regulation in Early Childhood*. London: The Guildford Press.

Brown, D. (1994) Play, the playground and the culture of childhood, in J. Moyles (ed.) *The Excellence of Play*. Buckingham: Open University Press.

Brown, S. and Cleave, S. (1990) *Four Year Olds in School: Meeting Their Needs*. Slough: NFER.

Brown, G. and Wragg, E.C. (1993) *Questioning*. London: Routledge.

Bruce, T. (1987) *Early Childhood Education*. Sevenoaks: Hodder and Stoughton.

Bruce, T. (1991) *Time to Play in Early Childhood Education*. Sevenoaks: Hodder and Stoughton.

Bruer, J.T. (1999) *The Myth of the First Three Years*. New York: The Free Press.

Bruner, J.S. (1966) *Toward a Theory of Instruction*. Cambridge, MA: Harvard University Press.

Bruner, J.S. (1977) Introduction, in B. Tizard and D. Harvey (eds) *The Biology of Play*. London: Spastics International Medical Publications.

Bruner, J.S. (1980) *Under Five in Britain: The Oxford Pre-school Research Project*. Oxford: Grant McIntyre.

Bruner, J.S. (1985) Vygotsky: a historical and conceptual perspective, in J.V. Wertsch (ed.) *Culture, Communication and Cognition: Vygotskian Perspective*. Cambridge: Cambridge University Press.

Bruner, J.S. (1986) *Actual Minds, Possible Worlds*. Cambridge, MA: Harvard University Press.

Bruner, J. and Haste, H. (eds) (1987) *Making Sense: The Child's Construction of the World*. London: Methuen.

Calderhead, J. and Miller, E. (1985) The integration of subject matter knowledge in student teachers' classroom practice. Conference paper, British Educational Research Association, Sheffield.

Calvin, W.H. (1996) *How Brains Think: Evolving Intelligence Then and Now*. London: Weidenfeld & Nicolson.

Campbell, R.J. and Neill, S.R.St.J. (1990) *Thirteen Hundred and Thirty Days: Final Report of a Pilot Study of Teacher Time in Key Stage 1, Commissioned by the Assistant Masters and Mistresses Association*. Warwick: University of Warwick, Department of Education.

Campbell, R.J., Evans, L., Neill, S.R.St.J. and Packwood, A. (1993) *The Use and Management of Infant Teachers' Time: Some Policy Issues*. Stoke-on-Trent: Trentham.

Carnegie Corporation of New York (1994) *Starting Points: Meeting the Needs of our Youngest Children*. New York: Carnegie Corporation.

Carr, W. and Kemmis, S. (1986) *Becoming Critical: Education, Knowledge and Action Research*. Lewes: Falmer Press.

Central Advisory Council for Education (CACE) (1967) *Children and their Primary Schools* (The Plowden Report). London: HMSO.

Chang, G.L. and Wells, G. (1988) The literate potential of collaborative talk, in M. Maclure, T. Phillips and A. Wilkinson (eds) *Oracy Matters*. Milton Keynes: Open University Press.

Clarricoates, K. (1983) Classroom interaction, in J. Whyld (ed.) *Sexism in the Secondary Curriculum*. London: Harper and Row.

Cohen, D. (1997) *The Secret Language of the Mind*. London: Duncan Baird.

Cousins, J. (1990) Are your little humpty dumpties floating or sinking? *Early Years*, 10 (2): 28–38.

Cousins, J. (1999) *Listening to Four Year Olds*. London: National Early Years Network.

Cox, C.B. and Boyson, R. (eds) (1975) *The Fight for Education: Black Paper 1975*. London: Dent.

Cox, C.B. and Boyson, R. (eds) (1977) *Black Paper 1977*. London: Maurice Temple Smith Ltd.

Cox, C.B. and Dyson, A.E. (eds) (1969a) *Fight for Education: A Black Paper*. London: Critical Quarterly Society.

Cox, C.B. and Dyson, A.E. (eds) (1969b) *Black Paper Two*. London: Critical Quarterly Society.

Cox, C.B. and Dyson, A.E. (eds) (1970) *Black Paper Three: Goodbye Mr Short*. London: Critical Quarterly Society.

Cox, T. and Sanders, S. (1994) *The Impact of the National Curriculum on the Teaching of Five-Year-Olds*. London: Falmer Press.

Curtis, A. (1994) Play in different cultures and different childhoods, in J. Moyles (ed.) *The Excellence of Play*. Buckingham: Open University Press.

Darling, J. (1994) *Child-Centred Education and its Critics*. London: Paul Chapman.

David, T., Curtis, A. and Siraj-Blatchford, I. (1992) *Effective Teaching in the Early Years: Fostering Children's Learning in Nurseries and in Infant Classes*. OMEP (UK). Stoke-on-Trent: Trentham.

Davies, W.J.K. (1987) *Towards Autonomy in Learning: Process or Product?* London: Council for Educational Technology.

Day, C. (1993) Reflection: a necessary but not sufficient condition for professional development, *British Educational Research Journal*, 19 (1): 83–93.

Department for Education and Employment (DfEE) (1998) *The National Literacy Strategy Framework*. London: DfEE.

Department for Education and Employment (DfEE) (1999) *The National Numeracy Strategy Framework*. London: DfEE.

Department for Education and Employment/Qualifications and Curriculum Authority (DfEE/QCA) (1998) *Desirable Outcomes for Children's Learning on Entering Compulsory Schooling*. London: DfEE Publications.

Department of Education and Science (DES) (1989) *The Education of Children Under Five*. London: HMSO.

Department of Education and Science (DES) (1990) *Starting with Quality* (The Rumbold Report). London: HMSO.

Dewey, J. (1933) *How We Think: A Restatement of the Relation of Reflective Thinking to the Educative Process*. Chicago, IL: Henry Regnery.

Dewey, J. (1938) *Experience and Education*. New York: Macmillan.

Diamond, M. and Hopson, J. (1998) *Magic Trees of the Mind*. New York: Dutton.

Dillon, J.T. (1981) To question or not to question during discussion, *Journal of Teacher Education*, 32 (5): 51–5.

Donaldson, M. (1978) *Children's Minds*. London: Fontana Press.

Donaldson, M. (1992) *Human Minds: An Exploration*. London: Penguin Books.

Dowling, M. (1995) *Starting School at Four: A Joint Endeavour*. London: Paul Chapman.

Dowling, M. (2000) *Young Children's Personal, Social and Emotional Development*. London: Paul Chapman.

Drummond, M.J. (1993) *Assessing Children's Learning*. London: David Fulton.

Drummond, M.J., Rouse, D. and Pugh, G. (1992) *Making Assessment Work*. Nottingham: NES Arnold/National Children's Bureau.

Dunn, J. (1988) *The Beginning of Social Understanding*. Oxford: Blackwell.

Early Years Curriculum Group (EYCG) (1992) *First Things First: Educating Young Children*. Oldham: Madeleine Lindley.

Early Years Curriculum Group (EYCG) (1995) *Four-Year-Olds in School: Myths and Realities*. Oldham: Madeleine Lindley.

Early Years Curriculum Group (EYCG) (1998) *Interpreting the National Curriculum at Key Stage 1: A Developmental Approach*. Buckingham: Open University Press.

Edwards, D. and Mercer, N. (1987) *Common Knowledge: The Development of Understanding in the Classroom*. London: Methuen.

Edwards, E. and Knight, P. (1994) *Effective Early Years Education: Teaching Young Children*. Buckingham: Open University Press.

Edwards, V. and Redfern, A. (1988) *At Home in School: Parent Participation in Primary Education*. London: Routledge.

Elfer, P. (1996) Building intimacy in relationships with young children in nurseries, *Early Years*, 16 (2): 30–4.

Entwhistle, N. (1987) *Understanding Classroom Learning*. Sevenoaks: Hodder and Stoughton.

Fein, G.G. (1981) Pretend play in childhood: an integrative review, *Child Development*, 52 (4): 1095–118.

Fisher, R. (1990) *Teaching Children to Think*. Oxford: Blackwell.

Fisher, J. (1996) Reflecting on the principles of early years practice, *Journal of Teacher Development*, 5 (1): 17–26.

Fisher, J. (1998a) Seen and heard, *Nursery World*, 5 February: 26–7.

Fisher, J. (1998b) All part of the plan, *Nursery World*, 12 February: 12–13.

Fisher, J. (1998c) For good measure, *Nursery World*, 19 February: 14–15.

Fisher, J. (1998d) Fit for the purpose? A critique of the National Framework for Baseline Assessment, *Education 3 to 13*, 26 (3): 9–14.

Fisher, J. (2000) The foundations of learning, *Early Education*, Summer.

Forman, E.A. and Cazden, C.B. (1985) Exploring Vygotskian perspectives in education: the cognitive value of peer interaction, in J.V. Wertsch (ed.) *Culture, Communication and Cognition: Vygotskian Perspective*. Cambridge: Cambridge University Press.

French, P. and Maclure, M. (1983) Teacher questions and pupil answers: an investigation of questions and answers in the infant classroom, in M. Stubbs and H. Hillier, *Readings in Language, Schools and Classrooms*, 2nd edn. London: Methuen.

Galton, M. and Patrick, H. (eds) (1990) *Curriculum Provision in Small Primary Schools*. London: Routledge.

Galton, M., Simon, B. and Croll, P. (1980) *Inside the Primary Classroom*. London: Routledge and Kegan Paul.

Galton, M. and Williamson, J. (1992) *Group Work and the Primary Classroom*. London: Routledge.

Gammage, P. (1999) After five, your brain is cooked, *Education Now*, summer (24).

Gardner, H. (1993) *The Unschooled Mind: How Children Think and How Schools Should Teach*. London: Fontana.

Garvey, C. (1977) *Play*. London: Fontana.

Gilbert, J.K. and Osborne, R.J. (1982) Studies of pupils' alternative frameworks or misconceptions in science, in W.F. Archenhold *et al.* (eds) *Cognitive Development Research in Science and Mathematics*. Leeds: University of Leeds.

Gipps, C.V. (1994) *Beyond Testing*. London: Falmer Press.

Gipps, C. and Stobart, G. (1993) *Assessment: A Teachers' Guide to Issues*. Sevenoaks: Hodder and Stoughton.

Greenfield, S. (1997) *The Human Brain: A Guided Tour*. London: Weidenfield & Nicolson.

Gura, P. (ed.) (1992) *Exploring Learning: Young Children and Blockplay*. London: Paul Chapman.

Hall, N. (1987) *The Emergence of Literacy*. Sevenoaks: Hodder and Stoughton.

Harlen, W. (ed.) (1985) *Primary Science ... Taking the Plunge*. Oxford: Heinemann Educational.

Hastings, N. and Schweiso, J. (1995) Tasks and tables: the effects of seating arrangements on task engagement in primary schools, *Educational Research* (NFER) 37 (3): 279–91.

Heath, S.R. (1983) *Ways with Words: Language, Life and Work in Communities and Classrooms*. Cambridge: Cambridge University Press.

Hohmann, M., Banet, B. and Weikart, D.P. (1979) *Young Children in Action*. Ypsilanti, MI: High/Scope Press.

Hohmann, M. and Weikart, D. (1995) *Educating Young Children*. Ypsilanti, MI: High/Scope Press.

Holt, J. (1982) *How Children Fail*, 2nd edn. Harmondsworth: Penguin.

Hughes, M. (1986) *Children and Number*. Oxford: Blackwell.

Hurst, V. (1994) Observing play in early childhood, in J. Moyles (ed.) *The Excellence of Play*. Buckingham: Open University Press.

Hurst, V. and Lally, M. (1992) Assessment and the nursery curriculum, in G.M. Blenkin and A.V. Kelly (eds) *Assessment in Early Childhood Education*. London: Paul Chapman.

Huskins, J. (1998) *From Disaffection to Social Inclusion*. Bristol: Jillich.

Inner London Education Authority (ILEA) (1990) *A Curriculum for Young Children: Outdoor Play*. London: Harcourt Brace Jovanovich.

Isaacs, S. (1968) *The Nursery Years*. London: Routledge and Kegan Paul.

Jenson, E. (1998) *Teaching with the Brain in Mind*. Alexandria, VA: ASCD.

Jones, N. (1989) Preface, in G. Barrett (ed.) *Disaffection From School? The Early Years*. Lewes: Falmer Press.

Jones, P. (1988) *Lipservice: The Story of Talk in Schools*. Milton Keynes: Open University Press.

Kagan, S. (1988) *Cooperative Learning: Resources for Teachers*. Riverside, CA: University of California.

Katz, L. (1998) Enhancing the formative years. Paper presented to the NAEIAC Early Years Conference, Oxford, June.

Kimberley, K. (1990) The third limb: assessment and the national curriculum, *The English Magazine*, 23, Summer: 19–26.

Kuhn, D. (2000) Theory of mind, metacognition, and reasoning: a lifespan perspective, in P. Mitchell and K.J. Riggs (eds) *Children's Reasoning and the Mind*. Hove: Psychology Press.

Lee, L. (1959) *Cider With Rosie*. London: Hogarth Press.

Lindon, J. (1993) *Child Development from Birth to Eight*. London: National Children's Bureau.

Lindsay, G., Lewis, A. and Phillips, E. (2000) *Evaluation of Accredited Baseline Assessment Schemes 1999–2000*. Warwick: University of Warwick, Psychology and Special Needs Research Unit.

Manning, K. and Sharp, A. (1977) *Structuring Play in the Early Years at School*. London: Ward Lock International.

Meadows, S. (1993) *The Child As Thinker: The Development and Acquisition of Cognition in Childhood*. London: Routledge.

Meighan, J. (1993) The hijack of young children's learning, in R. Meighan (ed.) *Theory and Practice of Regressive Education*. Nottingham: Educational Heretics Press.

Mortimore, P., Sammons, P., Stoll, L. and Ecob, R. (1986) *The Junior School Project*. London: ILEA.

Moss, P. and Penn, H. (1996) *Transforming Nursery Education*. London: Paul Chapman.

Moyles, J.R. (1989) *Just Playing? The Role and Status of Play in Early Childhood Education*. Milton Keynes: Open University Press.

Moyles, J.R. (1992) *Organising for Learning in the Primary Classroom*. Buckingham: Open University Press.

Moyles, J.R. (ed.) (1994) *The Excellence of Play*. Buckingham: Open University Press.

National Commission on Education (1993) *Learning to Succeed*. London: Heinemann.

Nutbrown, C. (1994) *Threads of Thinking*. London: Paul Chapman.

Office for Standards in Education (Ofsted) (1991) *Well Managed Classes in Primary Schools: Case Studies of Six Teachers*. London: DfE.

Office for Standards in Education (Ofsted) (1993a) *Curriculum Organisation and Classroom Practice in Primary Schools: A Follow-up Report*. London: DfE.

Office for Standards in Education (Ofsted) (1993b) *First Class: The Standards and Quality of Education in Reception Classes*. London: HMSO.

Office for Standards in Education (Ofsted) (1994a) *Assessing School Effectiveness*. London: Institute of Education.

Office for Standards in Education (Ofsted) (1994b) *Primary Matters: A Discussion on Teaching and Learning in Primary Schools*. London: HMSO.

Office for Standards in Education (Ofsted) (2000) *Inspecting Subjects 3–11: Guidance for Inspectors and Schools*. London: Ofsted.

Oxfordshire Early Years Team (1996) *Curriculum Matters 13: Early Years*. Oxford: Oxfordshire Education Department.

Pascal, C. (1990) *Under-Fives in the Infant Classroom*. Stoke-on-Trent: Trentham.

Pascal, C. and Ghaye, A. (1988) Four year old children in reception classrooms: participant perceptions and practice, *Educational Studies*, 14 (2): 187–208.

Phillips, T. (1988) On a related matter: why successful small-group talk depends upon not keeping to the point, in M. Maclure, T. Phillips and A. Wilkinson (eds) *Oracy Matters*. Milton Keynes: Open University Press.

Piaget, J. and Inhelder, B. (1956) *The Child's Conception of Space*. London: Routledge and Kegan Paul.

Pinker, S. (1997) *How the Mind Works*. London: Allen Lane, The Penguin Press.

Pollard, A. and Tann, S. (1993) *Reflective Teaching in the Primary School*, 2nd edn. London: Cassell.

Pollard, A., Broadfoot, P., Croll, P., Osborn, M. and Abbott, D. (1994) *Changing English Primary Schools? The Impact of the Education Reform Act at Key Stage One*. London: Cassell.

Postlethwaite, K. (1993) *Differentiated Science Teaching*. Buckingham: Open University Press.

Pringle, M.K. (1986) *The Needs of Children*, 3rd edn. London: Routledge.

Qualifications and Curriculum Authority (QCA) (1997) *Baseline Assessment Scales*. London: SCAA Publications.

Qualifications and Curriculum Authority/Department for Education and Employment (QCA/DfEE) (2000) *Curriculum Guidance for the Foundation Stage*. London: QCA.

Rabain-Jamin, J. (1989) Culture and early social interactions. The example of mother–infant object play in African and native French families, *European Journal of Psychology of Education*, 4 (2): 295–305.

Reid, J., Forrestal, P. and Cook, J. (1989) *Small Group Learning in the Classroom*. Scarborough, WA: Chalkface Press.

Richards, M. and Light, P. (1986) *Children of Social Worlds*. Cambridge: Polity Press.

Roberts, R. (1995a) *Self Esteem and Successful Early Learning*. London: Hodder and Stoughton.

Roberts, R. (ed.) (1995b) *A Nursery Education Curriculum for the Early Years*. Oxford: National Primary Centre.

Robinson, E.J. and Beck, S. (2000) What is difficult about counterfactual reasoning?, in P. Mitchell and K.J. Riggs (eds) *Children's Reasoning and the Mind*. Hove: Psychology Press.

Rose, C. and Nicholl, M.J. (1997) *Accelerated Learning for the 21st Century*. London: Judy Piatkus.

Rousseau, J.J. ([1762] 1976) *Emile* (translated by Barbara Foxley). London: Dent.

Rowland, S. (1984) *The Enquiring Classroom: An Introduction to Children's Learning*. Lewes: Falmer Press.

Rubin, K., Fein, G. and Vandenberg, B. (1983) Play, in E.M. Hetherington (ed.) *Manual of Child Psychology: Socialization, Personality and Development (Vol. IV)*. New York: Wiley.

Rutter, M. (1995) Clinical implications of attachment concepts, retrospect and prospect, *Journal of Child Psychology and Psychiatry*, 36 (4): 549–71.

School Curriculum and Assessment Authority (SCAA) (1995) *Planning the Curriculum at Key Stages 1 and 2*. London: SCAA.

School Curriculum and Assessment Authority (SCAA) (1997) *The National Framework for Baseline Assessment: Criteria and Procedures for the Accreditation of Baseline Assessment Schemes*. London: SCAA.

Schön, D.A. (1987) *Educating the Reflective Practitioner*. San Francisco, CA: Josey-Bass.

Schweinhart, L.J., Barnes, H. and Weikart, D.P. (1993) *Significant Benefits: The High/Scope Perry Preschool Study Through Age 27*. Ypsilanti, MI: High/Scope Press.

Sestini, E. (1987) The quality of the learning experiences of four year olds in nursery and infant classes, in NFER/SCDC (eds) *Four Year Olds in School*. Slough: NFER.

Shaffer, D.R. (1993) *Developmental Psychology: Childhood and Adolescence*, 3rd edn. Pacific Grove, CA: Brooks/Cole Publishing.

Sharp, C. (2000) When should children start school and what should we teach them?, *Topic*, 23, Spring.

Sinclair, J.McH. and Coulthard, R.M. (1975) *Towards an Analysis of Discourse: The English Used by Teachers and Pupils*. London: Oxford University Press.

Siraj-Blatchford, I. (1994) *The Early Years: Laying the Foundations for Racial Equality*. Stoke-on-Trent: Trentham Books.

Smith, A.B. (1993) Early childhood educare: seeking a theoretical framework in Vygotsky's work, *International Journal of Early Years Education*, 1 (1): 47–61.

Smith, H. (1995) *Unhappy Children*. London: Free Association Books.

Smith, P.K. and Cowie, H. (1991) *Understanding Children's Development*, 2nd edn. Oxford: Basil Blackwell.

Spender, D. (1982) *Invisible Women: The Schooling Scandal*. London: Writers and Readers.

Stanworth, M. (1981) *Gender and Schooling: A Study of Gender Divisions in the Classroom*. London: Women's Research and Resources Centre.

Stern, D. (1985) *The Interpersonal World of the Infant: A View from Psychoanalysis and Developmental Psychology*. New York: Basic Books.

Stevenson, C. (1987) The young four-year-old in nursery and infant classes: challenges and constraints, in NFER/SCDC (eds) *Four Year Olds in School*. London: NFER/SCDC.

Stodolsky, S.S., Ferguson, T.L. and Wimpelberg, K. (1981) The recitation persists; but what does it look like? *Journal of Curriculum Studies*, 13: 121–30.

Sutton-Smith, B. and Kelly-Byrne, D. (1984) The idealization of play, in P.K. Smith (ed.) *Play in Animals and Humans*. Oxford: Basil Blackwell.

Sylva, K. (1994) The impact of early learning on children's later development, Appendix C, in C. Ball (ed.) *Start Right: The Importance of Early Learning*. London: RSA.

Sylva, K. and Lunt, I. (1982) *Child Development: A First Course*. Oxford: Basil Blackwell.

Sylwester, R. (1995) *A Celebration of Neurons: An Educator's Guide to the Brain*. Alexandria, VA: ASCD.

Thomas, I. (1987) The Bedfordshire 4+ pilot scheme: some issues and implications, in NFER/SCDC (eds) *Four Year Olds in School*. Slough: NFER.

Tizard, B., Blatchford, D., Burke, J., Farquar, C. and Plewis, I. (1988) *Young Children at School in the Inner City*. Hove: Lawrence Erlbaum.

Tizard, B. and Hughes, M. (1984) *Young Children Learning: Talking and Thinking at Home and At School*. London: Fontana.

Tompkins, M. (1991) In praise of praising less, *Extensions* (newsletter of the High/Scope Curriculum), 6 (1): 1–3.

Vygotsky, L.S. (1962) *Thought and Language*. Cambridge, MA: MIT Press.

Vygotsky, L.S. (1966) Play and its role in the mental development of the child (translated by Catherine Mulholland), *Voprosy psikhologi*, 12 (6): 62–76.

Vygotsky, L.S. (1978) *Mind in Society: The Development of Higher Psychological Processes*. Cambridge, MA: Harvard University Press.

Warham, S.M. (1993) *Primary Teaching and the Negotiation of Power*. London: Paul Chapman.

Watson, R. (1998) Rethinking readiness for learning, in D. Olson and N. Torrance (eds) *Handbook of Education and Human Development: New Models of Learning, Teaching and Schooling*. London: Blackwell.

Wells, G. (ed.) (1981) *Learning Through Interaction*. Cambridge: Cambridge University Press.

Wells, G. (1985) *Language, Learning and Education*. Windsor: NFER/Nelson.

Wells, G. (1986) *The Meaning Makers: Children Learning Language and Using Language to Learn*. Sevenoaks: Hodder and Stoughton.

Whitehead, M. (1992) Assessment at Key Stage 1: core subjects and the developmental curriculum, in G.M. Blenkin and A.V. Kelly (eds) *Assessment in Early Childhood Education*. London: Paul Chapman Publishing.

Whitehead, M. (1993) Why not happiness? Reflections on change and conflict in early childhood education, in P. Gammage and J. Meighan (eds.) *Early Childhood Education: Taking Stock*. Ticknall: Education Now Publishing.

Willes, M.J. (1983) *Children Into Pupils: A Study of Language in Early Schooling*. London: Routledge and Kegan Paul.

Wolfe, P. and Brandt, R. (1998) What do we know from brain research? *Educational Leadership*. November: 8–13.

Wolfendale, S. (1993) *Baseline Assessment: A Review of Current Practice, Issues and Strategies for Effective Implementation*. OMEP (UK). Stoke-on-Trent: Trentham.

Wood, D. (1988) *How Children Think and Learn*. Oxford: Blackwell.

Wood, D., Bruner, J.S. and Ross, G. (1976) The role of tutoring in problem solving, *Journal of Child Psychology and Psychiatry*, 17 (2): 89–100.

Woods, P. (1990) *Teacher Skills and Strategies*. Basingstoke: Falmer Press.

INDEX

PROMOTING CHILDREN'S LEARNING FROM BIRTH TO FIVE
DEVELOPING THE NEW EARLY YEARS PROFESSIONAL

Angela Anning and Anne Edwards

- What sort of literacy and numeracy curriculum experiences are best suited to the needs of very young children?
- How can early years professionals bridge the current divisions between education and care to provide an approach to young children's learning which draws on the strengths of both traditions?
- How can these professionals be supported as they develop new practices which focus on young children as learners?
- What strategies are most effective in involving parents with their children's development in literacy and mathematical thinking?

Drawing upon research carried out in a range of early years settings, Angela Anning and Anne Edwards seek to address these questions. The emphasis throughout is upon enhancing the quality of children's learning and providing support for the practitioners who work with them. The complexity of addressing the various cognitive, social, physical and emotional learning needs of young children is discussed and practical strategies to develop children's learning are explored with a particular focus on communication and mathematical thinking. Published at a time of dramatic change in pre-school provision in the UK, the book will both inform and reassure early childhood professionals. It will be important reading for managers, administrators and all professionals working in early years and family services and an accessible text for those studying for childcare and education, and teaching qualifications.

Contents
Introduction – Setting the national scene – Integration of early childhood services – The inquiring professional – Young children as learners – Language and literacy learning – How adults support children's literacy learning – Mathematical learning – How adults support children's mathematical thinking – Creating contexts for professional development in educare – Early childhood services in the new millennium – Bibliography – Author index – Subject index.

192pp   0 335 20216 0 (Paperback)   0 335 20217 9 (Hardback)

StEPs: STATEMENTS OF ENTITLEMENT TO PLAY
A FRAMEWORK FOR PLAYFUL TEACHING
Janet Moyles and Siân Adams

The basis of this video and book Pack – StEPs – is a belief in the rights of the young child to appropriate opportunities to *be* children and to learn in playful and meaningful ways. It is also predicated upon a view that practitioners working with young children have equal rights to teach using playful strategies.

Children and adults are responsible for making the most of the playful learning and teaching opportunities provided in quality early childhood settings and to ensure that the curriculum – statutory or recommended – is implemented efficiently and effectively. The view taken throughout is that there is **no** conflict between being accountable to parents, politicians or providers for children's learning and offering play experiences as the basis for that learning.

Playful teaching and learning are discussed and exemplified throughout the two elements of the Pack. The video offers viewers a chance to see some of the practitioners who contributed to the Pack, in their own settings using aspects of StEPs to support their everyday teaching and learning. One of the major intentions of the Pack is that it should be used by practitioners and settings – or those undertaking training sessions with them – to both evaluate and extend play practices. The video, child development charts, planning sheets and other documentation, explained in various sections, support a variety of uses across a range of settings reflecting different backgrounds and ethos. Once the framework is understood, the StEPs themselves offer endless opportunities for development of quality learning experiences for children and for articulation, explanation and advocacy of quality practice by practitioners to parents, inspectors and those who evaluate settings.

Contents

112pp   0 335 20717 0   Paperback and Video Pack

SUPPORTING IDENTITY, DIVERSITY AND LANGUAGE IN THE EARLY YEARS

Iram Siraj-Blatchford and Priscilla Clarke

a valuable addition to what is developing into an impressive series of books on 'Supporting Early Learning'.

Nursery World

This excellent book should be required reading for every adult working with young children and for every student training to do so.

Early Education

The authors make a convincing case for the key role of early years practitioners, working closely with parents, carers and members of local communities, in supporting young children's development of positive dispositions towards themselves and others, regardless of differences and similarities.

Child Education

This book provides the main ingredients for professional development in working with young children in a diverse society. By helping children to develop a strong self-identity and good self-esteem we set the foundations for positive attitudes towards others and towards learning. Practical advice, real examples and staff activities bring the book to life. The book provides clear evidence and practical guidance on how to develop young children's emerging language, especially those children who have English as an additional language, and how to generate, activate and assess curriculum for diversity. Each chapter offers a clear combination of theory and practice and ends with excellent staff development activity and further readings. The book will be important reading for all students and practitioners working with young children.

Contents

Identity, self-esteem and learning – Language acquisition and diversity – Learning English as an additional language – Diversity and the curriculum – Parents as partners – Planning and evaluating for equity and diversity – Resources – References – Index.

160pp   0 335 20434 1 (Paperback)   0 335 20435 X (Hardback)